What readers say about *Refugee* . . .

. . . an amazing tale of survival amidst harsh and unforgiving circumstances.

. . . a personal tale which puts a face on the stories we hear about refugees and migrants moving from land to land. . . . my grandfather was Hungarian, and my father lived in Czechoslovakia, whose borders were changed repeatedly, similar to what Varda describes.

. . . not so much an account of the emotional impact on an individual as it is a lesson on the disruption to the civilian populace when high government redraws borders.

. . . portrays the impact that the unsettled times of the 1940s and 1950s in Eastern Europe had on people.

Throughout the ages, telling stories has been a way to pass down gifts from one generation to the next, a ritual of memories and tradition. Teaching through stories, whether at the Passover table or in the waiting room, is a way to connect: it reminds us of our bonds as human beings.
— Louise DeSalvo, *Writing as a Way of Healing* (1999)

REFUGEE

A TRUE STORY OF
COMING OF AGE IN A WAR ZONE

by

LUKACS JOHN VARDA

as told to
Janice Stensrude

"This war is not as in the past; whoever occupies a territory also imposes his own system as far as his army can reach. It cannot be otherwise." — Stalin (1945)

White Hair Press
Parker, Colorado
USA

REFUGEE
A True Story of Coming of Age in a War Zone
Copyright © 2023 by Lukacs John Varda
All rights reserved.

ISBN 979-8-9879244-0-2
White Hair Press

Book Design by Janice Stensrude
Cover by Dan Kwarcinski

Printed and distributed by Lulu.com

Dedicated

to all those through the centuries and into the present who have been forced from their homes by territorial ambitions

and

to my parents who saw their young family through one of the world's great wars. Though my father's spirit was crushed under the authoritarian heel of communism, my mother, small in stature but great in spirit, became the guiding force that brought her children to adulthood as useful adults.

Contents

Foreword	vii
Preface	ix
1. In the Beginning	1
2. A Community of Family	6
3. Escape from Bácska	16
4. The Road to Bátaszék	21
5. Zala	26
6. Occupation in the Promised Land	34
7. Time To Be a Kid	40
8. School Days	48
9. Communist Youth Leader	53
10. A Revolution	56
11. Again a Refugee	62
12. Sheltering in Italy	70
13. Sailing for Australia	76
14. The Final Refuge	80
15. Strangers in a Strange Land	89

Foreword

Lukacs John Varda's life narrative makes an essential contribution to the body of seldom-heard voices of those who have lived at the mercy of rulers and dictators who sought to control even history. Born into a family of Hungarian Székely nobility, John's life has been neither privileged nor wealthy. When he was an infant, his family was reduced to poverty by an accidental fire that destroyed the paper-money wealth of the entire community of Bukovina Székely, who were settled in the remote mountains of Moldavia. Shortly after, in accordance with an international treaty, his tribe were relocated to an area in Yugoslavia that is currently part of Serbia, a location that soon proved to be just another temporary home.

Six years old and already twice a refugee, he now faced the most physically and emotionally demanding of his family's moves to another hoped-for permanent home, a journey that was to take more than seven months, stopping and starting along the way. At each and every one of these territorial relocations, John's family were participating witnesses in the transnational power shifts that determined where and how they would live.

From the ages of eight to nineteen, John was a first-hand witness to the Communist experiment, as Hungary's Russian liberators became their totalitarian masters. He remembers the hardships of being a farm family forced into the collective by high taxes and the ever-present fear of even whispering disapproval of the government. He obeyed the advice of the kind collective farm chairman who had recruited him to oversee a recreation program for the collective's young people: 'This is the world we live in. Let's make the best of it.' And that's what he did.

In 1956, after briefly participating in that year's unsuccessful revolution against the Communist government, he was yet to face further hunger, deprivation and sometimes abuse in refugee camps before finding his way to Australia, his final refuge.

Throughout history, the lives of ordinary citizens have fallen victim to tyrants addicted to the intoxicating power of territorial expansion. The voices of those who have lived these historic moments at grass roots are history's only hope to come closer to the truth. For by knowing and beginning to understand the good and the bad of our truth, our experiments in living may come closer and closer to a state of respectful humanity.

Lukacs John Varda is one of those voices.

Janice Stensrude
Editor
Parker, Colorado USA
January 2023

Preface

I escaped from Hungary the 14th of January 1957, my nineteenth birthday. I went through hell during the period that followed, and a year later, the 14th of January 1958, on my twentieth birthday, I first stepped onto Australian soil when I went ashore in the old port city of Fremantle in Western Australia. We continued on to Melbourne, where I finally arrived on the 20th of January 1958.

After being in Australia for over thirty years, I finally went back to Hungary for a visit. I enjoyed every minute of it. I was surprised how much my people achieved in the environment where we settled, most of us in Bátaszék. Like my parents, the others also started with nothing. Lots of books have now been written of our forced immigration from Madefalva to Bukovina to Yugoslavia to Bátaszék—and, in my case, back to Yugoslavia, then Italy and, finally, Australia.

In Australia, my friends and others close to me often say that I, too, have a story to tell. We'll see how I go. I will try to deal with a bit of history, a bit of everything else. If I'm not completely correct, well, I'm writing mostly what I have read and what I remember. Most of it happened a long, long time ago.

1

In the Beginning

I remember crying and being hungry all the time. It was 1944. I was six years old and it was not the first time I had been a refugee. My family has a long history of being refugees, though those earliest times were not within the personal memory of my parents, or even my grandparents.

There are many stories (and a number of scholarly theories), but the favourite story among my ancestors was that we are descended from Attila the Hun. According to that legend, after Attila died and his empire crumbled, Attila's favourite son, Prince Csaba, led the surviving Huns first to safety in Transylvania, then returned east with them to Scythia, between the Caspian Sea and the Black Sea, where Huns and Magyars merged into one people. The Huns who chose to stay behind in Transylvania, so the story goes, are my people, the Székely.

Like other tribal groups, my ancestors' fortunes waxed and waned with the fortunes of their allies and the whims of queens, kings, emperors and other moguls. From their legendary beginnings in the fifth century and into the eighteenth century, the Székely negotiated a place of honour among those who seized and wielded power. In those early days, in exchange for allegiance and services as border guards, we paid no taxes.

In 1764, it was Maria Theresa, the Austrian queen, who held power. She had made for herself an empire that included all of Hungary and most of Transylvania. Maria Theresa did not honour the old pacts, and when Székely youth fled in great numbers to avoid conscription into her army (where they would be expected to serve as long as twelve years), the commanders of the imperial army, in a punitive action borne of frustration and rage, slaughtered hundreds of women and children in the Székely village of Mádéfalva.

When the dust had settled, one thousand Székely had fled into neighbouring Moldavia. It was this cruel and impetuous action by the armies of the Empress Maria Theresa that became the defining event for the people who are known today as the Bukovina Székely, the people among whom I was born.

I need to pause for a moment to confess that this version of history is not accepted by everyone. In today's Hungary, the official history states that the Székely rebelled and declared war on the Austrian Empire and that only soldiers lost their lives. It was such a long time ago, and it really shouldn't matter. Yet my tribe continue to repeat the old history. A monument, built in the early twentieth century and inscribed as a memorial to those who died in the 'Mádéfalva Massacre', still stands today where the conflict occurred, in what is now a commune in Romania.

There is a story in our family that our ancestor, Titus Varda, was a friend of General Andrew Hadik, an influential member of Maria Theresa's army. Titus, so our family story says, undertook the long and treacherous journey to Vienna, where he begged his friend to intercede for the badly treated Székely. General Hadik thus began a long period of negotiations on our behalf. Eventually, the Empire reclassified the

Mádéfalva incident, from rebellion to misunderstanding. The Székely, the General reasoned, had not refused to serve, but rather believed they had a contract in place as border guards and therefore were already serving the Empire.

Thus, some twenty or so years after the events at Mádéfalva, the Austro-Hungarian Empire offered my tribe land in Bukovina, that part of the Moldavian heartland that was annexed by the Empire. The government built a new house for each family, and five new villages were formed, an island of Hungarian Székely culture in a land mostly populated by Romanians. The new communities were named Jószeffalva (Joseph Town), Hadikfalva (Hadik Town), Andrásfalva (Andrew Town), Istensegits (God Help Us!), and Fogadjisten (Accept God's Will!). The naming of these last two reflected the hopeful attitude of that generation of refugees.

The growing Székely population could not thrive indefinitely on the limited land of the five villages, and many Bukovina Székely migrated to Transylvania, Canada and Brazil. At one point the Hungarian government resettled 4,000 Székely in Bácska in the south of Hungary. Then, during the Great War, Austria-Hungary aligned itself with Germany. The winners punished the losers by seizing territory and rewarded their allies by dividing it among them. It was through this redistribution of Austro-Hungarian lands in 1918 that Bukovina and Transylvania became part of the modern state of Romania.

Through it all, my family stayed in Bukovina, and I was born there in 1938 in the village of Jószeffalva. Times had not always been easy, but, at the time of my birth, the homes guaranteed us by our eighteenth-century persecutors-turned-benefactors had been ours for more than 150 years.

The Hungarians in Bácska, including our Székely relatives, had not been so fortunate. In the territorial reshuffling that followed World War I, Bácska had become part of the new nation of Yugoslavia. Forced from their homes by the terms of the surrender, Hungarians escaped across the new borders or were placed in concentration camps. By the time the rumble of World War II was beginning to be heard, Bácska was the home of Serbian farmers, who had claimed the land with their labour.

In 1941, the Hungarian government allied itself with Hitler's Germany and, in a new wave of nationalistic expansion, snatched Bácska from Yugoslavia and immediately began to re-Hungarianize the area. At the same time, in accordance with a treaty between Hungary and Romania, all five of our villages in Bukovina, 13,200 souls, gave up our property, possessions and Romanian citizenship in exchange for our repatriation with our Hungarian homeland. It was a mixed blessing. We were leaving behind everything we had worked for, everything we had ever known, for the promise of a better life, freed from our minority status in Romania. Many Székely thought it was the answer to our prayers. It was not, however, the answer to the prayers of the Serbian farmers in southern Bácska who were forced from their homes to make way for our 'homecoming'. Again, those who held power redrew borders and shuffled the populace like so many game pieces.

As for me, I continue to think of it as my first personal experience as a refugee, though I was too young to remember. We could not take with us any livestock, farm implements or basic household furniture, but some brought along a trunk of family mementos or a special chair or a chest. For the most part, we had only our clothing. Everything we were leaving behind was to be replaced when we arrived in Bácska. We knew well in advance our time and day of departure. Knowing my mother, I think she must have cleaned the house from top to bottom, so that the new owners would appreciate the sort of people who had first lived there. When the day and hour of departure arrived, the Bukovina Székely closed the doors of their homes. With infants and their few belongings in their arms, they reported to the railway stations where we boarded boxcars headed for Bácska.

Our resettlement was not for long. Barely three years later, late on an autumn afternoon, my family learned the Serbs were coming to reclaim their farms. We had twenty minutes to gather what we could and run.

2

A Community of Family

My father's family—his parents, his three brothers and seven sisters and all their children—were our family, our friends and our community. My cousins were my companions and playmates. Being lonely was never an option.

My clearest memory of my grandfather, Antal Varda, is standing between his legs as he told me stories. That would have been in Bácska shortly before his death in 1943. I was too young to have memories of the times in Jószeffalva, but I still have memories of the house in Bácska that he shared with his wife, my Grandmother Rozália. I particularly remember a picture that hung on their wall. It was a man on horseback, wearing the uniform of a *huszár* in the Napoleonic army, his saber at his side. His facial features were obstructed by a dense pattern of black ink scribbles. I had many romantic notions about the identity of this mysterious headless man, but none were more romantic than the truth. Grandmother Rozália's father had served with Napoleon's elite light cavalry regiment of hussars during his tragic Russian campaign. History tells us that Great Grandfather was indeed fortunate to have survived the Russian winter and make it home to marry his sweetheart. It was explained to me that others in the family had served on the side of the Russians, and the picture had been defaced to protect the family from those who would have considered him to be a traitorous enemy.

It was tradition in my father's family that the youngest son took care of aged parents. So when Grandmother Rozália was widowed in 1943, she went to live with Uncle Frank, my father's youngest brother. As it turned out, Uncle Frank's wife didn't think much of the family tradition. I think it was 1949—I remember it was winter—when a deeply hurt Grandmother Rozália came to live with us. Mom and Dad gave her a small room of her own behind the kitchen. After her arrival, the family of my childhood, as I remember it, was complete.

Every time Grandmother Rozália lay down to rest or sleep, she would begin coughing. I don't remember anyone saying what was wrong with her, but despite medicines from the doctor and every folk remedy the family could think of, she coughed like that for the rest of her life.

She dressed all in black, as was the custom of the time—a long black skirt, black blouse and black jacket. She was a tiny woman and very thin, but she could wield a mean wooden spoon. I remember Dad teasing her. He would pick her up and give her a big kiss, and she would beat him with her big wooden spoon until he put her down. He would be laughing the whole time. Grandmother Rozália and Mom got along well, and she was with us until her death in 1952.

My father's family were all farmers, but there were not so many farmers on my mother's side. Her father had been a railway station master. Though he owned a farm, it was tended by hired laborers. After his retirement, he was often called back as a relief station master at various railway stations. I think he was seventy when he completely stopped doing that work.

My mother's family was not so large as my father's, but big enough. Her five sisters and two brothers had settled their families in other towns thirty and forty kilometers distant from Bátaszék. Hers was my holiday family. Once a year, at Easter or Christmas, we would travel to the home of my maternal grandmother, where most of my mother's family would be gathered to celebrate together. These were times of great fun, with dozens and dozens of cousins to play with. It was during these family get-togethers that we kids would sometimes hear, by chance, snippets of gossip about neighbours and family. That's how I learned about Uncle Albert, my mother's oldest brother.

Like his father before him, Uncle Albert worked for the railroad and became a station master. He came to many of these family gatherings without his wife. Aunt Marta had rejected the Catholic faith of her childhood and converted to Jehovah's Witness. Uncle Albert and Aunt Marta had what the adults described as an on-again-off-again marriage. At least twice, she converted back to Catholicism, then back to Witness. During her non-Catholic periods, she refused marital intimacy and even all outward signs of affection towards her husband. It couldn't have been that her new religion required celibacy. After all, there were many children among the Witnesses. I think maybe Uncle Albert's powers of persuasion were most potent in the bedroom, and she feared that her feelings for her husband would seduce her into returning to a religion that she no longer felt was true. Aunt Marta had somehow found a religion that promised greater guilt and more terrifying consequences from sin than Catholicism.

One of the basic beliefs of Aunt Marta's new religion was that it was sinful to celebrate birthdays or holidays that originated with 'false' religions, which was every religion except their own. Maybe things would not have been quite so bad if both her on-again-off-again religions had not been so insistent that they alone were the One Great Truth. But they did. So when Aunt Marta wore her Jehovah's Witness hat, she refused to attend our family holiday dinners, which she viewed as religious holiday celebrations of a false religion. No doubt the family was put off by being shunned. There was further anguish years later when my cousin Peter, who converted with his mother, was imprisoned by the Communists for refusing to serve in the army. His religion demanded that he could serve no government, as his church was his *only* authority. It was an unhappy life for Uncle Albert, the family gossip said, but he would not join Aunt Marta in her new religion.

I know nothing about my great grandparents on my mother's side. But on my father's side, my great grandfather was a judge and quite well to do. Many of the Székely who had emigrated to Canada and America would send dollars to their relatives in Bukovina. Since there was no bank, it was my great grandfather who converted these dollars to local currency. And because there was no bank, the family's liquid assets were kept in a large chest in their house. When Great Grandfather died, the responsibilities of village 'banker' fell to Grandfather Antal. I don't know if he had any official title, but I remember that letters addressed to him had 'Esquire' after his name. My father was his eldest son, and as was our tradition, Dad expected one day to inherit the wealth that his father had inherited before him. God had other plans.

It was 1939 and it would have been autumn, because the men were harvesting and Mom had gone to the fields to take Dad his lunch. Even today, some people grumble that it was a hate crime against 'those Hungarians', but the official story is that two boys had built a fire outdoors to make popcorn. They were holding the large saucer-shaped sieve, filled with dried popping corn, over the open fire when a sudden wind arose, carrying sparks to a nearby house. The thatched roof immediately caught fire, and with each gust of wind the fire spread from one house to the next. Mom told me that I was asleep under their bed, tucked away in the carved wooden cradle that was used for making bread when there was no baby in the house. I don't remember who they say rescued me, perhaps Grandmother Rozália. She and Grandfather Antal lived in the house next to us.

No one died in the fire, but most of our town burned to the ground. Our family lost everything except our land and the clothes on our backs. The chest with its contents that represented our accumulated family wealth was completely consumed by the flames. That fire was a great equalizer. We were no longer affluent citizens, but as poor as the poorest farmers among the Bukovina Székely.

Through the years of hardship and his bouts of drinking, my father spewed resentment for having lost his inheritance. I don't think he ever got over it.

In his younger years, my father was very active and playful. I remember very fondly the time he built a huge swing out of wood in our front yard. Sitting on his lap on that swing, I was full of happiness and terror all at the same time. I remember watching him many times stand up on the swing and force it so high that it would go right around. Sometimes he would stop at the very top upside down, suspended for a few seconds. I would hold my breath in amazement and fear, but he never fell off.

Dad loved a good time, dancing and drinking and celebrating with family and friends. He and Mom were members of the Székely dance troop. In 1938, when they danced for the governor in Budapest, Dad was the lead dancer. Mom was pregnant with me, so a substitute danced in her place.

Dad was much older than Mom and very jealous. She was always careful to keep her gaze straight ahead lest she be accused of looking at another man. I sometimes wonder if he was really jealous or if it was just an act. When Mom nagged him about his drinking, he would say it was because she was an unfaithful wife, always looking at other men. This always succeeded in turning the conversation from his drinking to his fears of her infidelity. She would protest her innocence over and over, forgetting her anger at his coming home drunk, concerned only that he believe her innocence. It would be hard to give up a jealousy that worked so well to his advantage.

Dad's first wife had died quite young, and they had only one child, my half sister, Apalonia. She was three years old when my mother and father married. My mother was herself still a teenager. Apalonia seemed never to recover from the loss of her mother. Throughout her childhood and teen years, she would run off to her aunt, her mother's sister, and sometimes live there for weeks or months. Until the day she died, Mom carried a deep sadness that she had never formed with Apalonia the mother's bond that she thought her situation had demanded of her.

I was my mother's first born in 1938. In 1939 she suffered a stillbirth, then gave birth to my brother Antal in 1940. Antal died from whooping cough before I had a memory of his existence. I heard my mother tell the story of his death many times.

'He died five times,' she would say, each time with the same grief in her voice. 'We covered his head because we thought he was dead, and ten minutes later we would hear again a cough.'

It was like the story of the prodigal son in the Bible. The lost child was the most precious.

When my sister Teréz was born in Bácska in 1941, someone else in the family named her Anne without consulting with my mother. Mom was so angry that she refused to feed the baby until the name was changed. Afterwards, she felt ashamed. Every illness Terry had, every problem that arose, Mom blamed on herself, and she protected her from everything. Terry was afraid of animals, and when Dad wanted her to guide the horses, she would refuse. Dad thought she would get over her fear if she were made to work with the animals. Mom thought he was being unreasonable, and this was one of the things that they fought over time and again.

My sister Veronika was born in Bácska in 1944. And then there were no more children.

Dad's drinking became more frequent and Mom's disappointed anger more evident. It was not so bad at first. He would come home in a jolly mood, after going missing for hours and hours, and throw his arms around Mom, sometimes succeeding in planting a long kiss full on her lips, but more frequently being pushed away before his lips so much as glanced her face.

She would say, 'Go away. You stink!'

Then he would stumble off to bed, sometimes giving me a wink as he wobbled away.

The drinking must have been there when they married, but perhaps Mom thought it would get better, or maybe Dad's preoccupation with his new teenage bride temporarily distracted him from his favourite pastime of sharing drink, laughter and good conversation. Some people grow more tolerant of alcohol as they consume more and more, progressively needing larger and larger amounts to achieve a state of alcohol-induced bliss. Dad's pattern was the opposite. As time went by, it took less and less to bring him to a stupor.

As early as I can remember, there had been binges. Dad was clever and creative, a jack of all trades. He did handiwork for friends and neighbours and was paid with sausage, ham and other food stuffs. He would leave the house to repair a neighbour's plough or visit a brother or sister, then a neighbourly drink or two would inspire other stops and other drinks. Somewhere along the way, he got lost in a seductive continuum of drink, unaware of how long he had been away from home. Days later, he would appear, move silently to the bedroom and sleep all day, sometimes for two days. His hangover could last for days. He would retch continually, unable to even keep down a glass of water.

As I reached the age of eight, I began to pick up some of the work and share it with Mom. As I grew up I had less and less respect for him. Many times my teacher would come to me in school and ask if I knew where they could find my mom. Dad had been found—again—sleeping at the side of the road, and they were afraid he might have been hit. Of course, they didn't really think he had been hit, they were just trying to save my feelings. So I couldn't wait to get old enough to leave home.

When he was sober, he was the best father a boy can have. So when I lived at home I had that love and hate feeling for him. It is still very painful to think about those years.

Mom had always blamed Dad for everything. She even blamed him for my leaving. Over the years, his bitterness and his drinking drove a wedge between the two of them. She would not even visit his grave many years after his death. In the last few years before her death, she came to see her part in her marital problems. She said that she had been young and stupid.

In a community as small as ours, I'm certain someone must have reported to Mom where he had been when he was gone. But I never heard. The silence between Mom and Dad when he awoke from one of those benders cast a veil of silence over everything. It was like the silence of new snowfall, but without the fresh exhilaration. It was heavy and sat on our chests like layers of winter rugs. He must have promised it would never happen again, for a few days later things returned to normal, and indeed, for many months he would not take a drink. Then he would begin again. First only a drink or two with family, and then one day he would disappear, again returning days later—dirty, contrite and helplessly hung over.

It was about 1950 when Mom threatened to leave, and this time he believed her. He went to the priest, who arranged for him to enter a sanitarium for ninety days. He began to attend church regularly and became good friends with the priest. I remember the church tower clock had stopped, and no one had been able to repair it. Dad spent a good while examining it, figuring out how it worked and what went wrong. He discovered a damaged chain and devised a way to mend it.

He was always interested in learning new things. He even took up basketmaking a few years before he died. He wove them with willow strips. Soon he had a queue of people waiting to buy his baskets. No one in our family was ever able to claim one before it was sold.

His period of sobriety abruptly ended six months after he had completed his treatment. I don't know what happened. It was probably nothing significant. He may have been helping someone with repairs and just decided it would be okay to accept the offered drink, just to see how it went. Before long, though, he had resumed his old pattern, and as time went on, things grew worse. His tolerance for alcohol became less and less until one glass of wine would make him drunk. At first I thought he was dodging work, but then I realized he suffered debilitating hangovers after only a small amount of wine.

Drink had changed him. I no longer recognized the father of my early childhood. In the last few years before I left home, I saw that my mother had become a single parent, bitterly nursing the handicapped child my father had become, and doing her best to be both father and mother to my sisters and me. She grew to hate the odors of strong drink and tobacco smoke. In later years, Uncle Frank once had a smoke in her kitchen, and she took to cooking outdoors until the smell and all memory of it had gone.

Dad was definitely one of those people who became a new man when he had a drink; and as the old joke goes, then the new man needed to have a drink. He always denied that he had a 'drinking problem'. He just enjoyed having a drink with friends, he would say.

3

Escape from Bácska

The village church was the centre of our social and political lives, as had been the custom across Europe for centuries. The priests kept careful records of births, deaths and marriages, entering them in their tall, neatly lined ledger journals. Our church served a civic as well as a religious function; it was a liaison between us and our national government. So it was not unusual that our priest was the one to deliver important news about the war. I don't know why, but on that one particular day, my parents did not know that the priest had called everyone to the church.

It was sundown, the 7th of October, 1944. Mom had just slopped the pigs and was tossing feed to the chickens when I saw the policeman approach her. I could not hear what they were saying, but I saw Mom's hands fly to her face, something I had seen her do before when the news she was receiving was either very good or very bad. They did not talk long before the policeman hurried off. I stood by the door and watched as she tossed the last bit of grain at the chickens and ran towards the house. She hurried to the back of the house, collected my baby sister Veronika from her bed and called to me and my sister Térez to follow.

'We're going to see Grandmother Rozália,' she said.

Terry and I followed her through the rows of corn that separated our back door from the back door of Dad's brother, our Uncle Frank, where Grandmother Rozália was living. The stalks were taller than Mom and full with ready-to-pick ears. The silks of the topmost ears fluttered above our heads in the autumn breeze. Mom kept too vigorous a stride for me to be able to hop or skip or jump up to shake a stalk and watch the corn silk wiggle. Terry and I could do nothing more than hurry along behind, scurrying to keep up.

It was many years later that I learned what the policeman had said, that he had come to warn us that the Serbian Chetniks were only a few kilometers away. Not knowing about the meeting at the church where everyone else had heard the news, we were among the last of the families to learn of the danger. We reached Uncle Frank's house, only to find that Dad was not there and no one knew where he was. Everyone was rushing about, packing wagons and preparing for a hurried leavetaking.

I could feel the fear mounting in Mom as we headed back across the cornfield towards our house. She was walking even more quickly than before, and Terry and I struggled to keep up. Suddenly there was a noise at the edge of the cornfield behind us. Mom screamed and began running. Terry attached herself to Mom's free hand, and I desperately grasped a handful of skirt in an attempt to keep up. Her skirt carried me along, three steps on the ground, two steps in the air. Terry was swinging from Mom's hand, now and then her foot making contact with the ground. Mom screamed and cried, and we all screamed with her, baby Vera letting loose the loudest and most terrifying wails of all.

As we approached our house, it became clear that no one was following through the cornfield. I felt safer back in the house, Terry and

I crowding into our mother's skirt. Mom's sobs became controlled sniffs, and then the calm silence of someone with work to do. Breaking free of our huddle, Mom put the still-wailing Vera into her cot and turned to her work.

Since the heavy work of the farm was ended for the year and there were bills to pay, Dad had sold our beautiful pair of horses and bought an old, but still somewhat serviceable, grey workhorse. So it was Old Grey that Mom hitched to our wagon, which she frantically began to pack full, making one trip after another from house to wagon. She sent Terry and me off in one direction or another to get some bit of something, keeping us occupied as she worked. Sometimes she would burst into stifled sobs, and Terry and I would cry with her.

There was finally no more room in the wagon. Baby Vera was tucked into a makeshift cradle of blankets behind the wagon seat, and Mom lifted Terry and me up, where we wedged ourselves among bags stuffed with clothing, loose tools and kitchenware, and the boxes she had used to pack two young pigs and some chickens. She pulled the heavy cotton cover tight over the bent-willow staves, then tied one of the goats to the wagon. Before hoisting herself into the wagon seat, she opened the door to the corn shed and opened front and back gates so the animals left behind could forage for themselves.

Darkness was falling as our wagon took to the road. I looked back to see our two cows, the other goat and four grown pigs going about their day's business, untouched by the terror and uncertainty that disturbed our mother. Had it not been for Mom's tear-streaked face and periodic frightened sobs, Terry and I would have found it a great adventure to be taking a wagon ride midst the sounds of squealing pigs and clucking hens.

It must have been cloudy or dark of the moon, or both, for soon it was pitch black and we were alone on the road. Perhaps the horse could see, but we couldn't. Over the horizon, we saw flashes, sometimes barely visible, sometimes large enough to momentarily light our way—and always, they were followed by explosions. One might be barely audible, the next so loud a boom that we thought it must be exploding beside us. Much later we learned that the rail station had been bombed, cutting off an escape route for many who had jammed into the rail cars. Among them were my mother's brother and his young family. As a railroad employee working in the town, he did not own a horse and had no way to escape with his family. They were interned by the Serbs and held in a concentration camp. It was as recent as the 1990s that they were compensated for being 'illegally interned'.

We had finally reached the main road and had been going for some time when we began to hear sounds of movement, gradually becoming clearer and clearer, until we could discern the clop, clop, clopping of horse hooves and the shuffling noises of people walking. I could feel Mom's relief as we caught up to a group that included one of Dad's sisters and one of his brothers. She felt safer, self-consciously wiping her streaked face and greeting them with a faint smile of happy recognition. No one seemed in fear of pursuit as we set up camp at the side of the road.

When I awoke, it was daylight. I saw Mom giving hay and corn to our horse. There was a feeling of taking stock, of things being properly organized after our hurried departure. Uncle Stefan killed the two little pigs and Mom killed the chickens. She cooked the fresh meat on an open fire and packed it into pots to be eaten later, then inspected the foot of our limping goat. The hard, uneven surface of the gravel road had caused a painful sore. Mom set the poor thing free. On its own, it had a chance for recovery.

Traffic on the road became heavier and heavier as our traveling group extinguished camp fires and packed wagons. We were moving onto the highway when a truck stopped near us, and Dad jumped off. We all felt safer then. Hearing of the warnings, he had come as fast as he could from the neighbouring village where he had been visiting a sister. We were gone by the time he arrived at our house, and he had hid himself in a hay stack to escape the notice of the angry Chetniks.

Thirty-five years later, my sisters and I drove to Bácska, but nothing remained to remind us that we had ever been there. Even the little graveyard where our family were buried was wiped from existence. The only monument to that short chapter in our young lives was a vast field of grain, bright green in the afternoon sun.

4

The Road to Bátaszék

The day after we ran for our lives, Hungary withdrew from Bácska, and the German army was looking for an escape route. But my family and the others were not just running away. They were running towards another promise of a better future. The priest had told us to make our way to the town of Bátaszék in the province of Tolna, where the Hungarian government promised new homes. This was not like our move from Bucovina to Bácska. There were no railway cars, no real organization. To my young eyes, there were millions on the highways, soldiers going in one direction on one side of the road, others advancing in the opposite direction on the other side—and along the verges, lines of refugees going north on one side and south on the other. Through this two-way flow of human lava, the Soviets and Germans were at combat on the ground and the English and Americans were striking from the air, trying to stop the German retreat.

We traveled north on the right side of the road with all the other Bácska refugees. Just as many people were traveling south on the left side, and in the middle were German army tanks and every other variety of military and civilian vehicle. Aeroplanes circled overhead, some so low that we could see the faces of the pilots as they strained to isolate a military target. It soon became instinctive to seek cover whenever we saw a fighter descending. The air would be heavy with the sounds of terrified women screaming in panic and children crying in response as we ran to the side of the road. 'Get down, get down,' the men would shout, hiding their own fear behind the masks of their family authority.

There were thousands of soldiers, most of them German, traveling on foot in the opposite direction. They looked in terrible condition, and some had bad injuries. Every few hundred meters, we would come upon the sight of a burned-out truck or tank, sometimes littered with dead bodies, in the open fields that lined the roadway. No one stopped to look.

Far above us, we could see hundreds of bombers going in one direction, then coming back in the other direction a short time later. The ground trembled from the enormous noise they made. Across the ocean six-year-old boys were preparing for their days of school and play, and I was on an open highway with a sea of people, so scared about what was going to happen to us.

We had to stop often to give our old horse food and water. Sometimes she would stop on her own, refusing to move. Dad did not have the heart to hit her or urge her on, as some were doing to their horses in their urgent fear to keep moving. He would stroke her, pat her, whisper encouragement and affection and give her the time she wanted to eat, drink and take a rest.

The road was narrow and paved with rough, sharp-edged gravel. On either side was a verge for pedestrians and horses, bordered by a deep drainage ditch, interrupted by an occasional culvert pipe. The pipe was paved over with earth and turf, giving access to the road from the open field. People behind us would often get angry when we stopped. It was impossible for them to pass us, caught between the deep ditch on their right and the constant traffic flow of military vehicles on their left, in the center of the road. Over and over, we pulled off the road at a culvert to give the horse a rest. Each time, we grew farther and farther behind our people.

There were days when we hardly moved, brought to a standstill by heavy traffic and air raids. Sometimes word would pass down to us from several kilometers ahead that fighter planes were peppering German troops with machine-gun fire. The dead, the wounded, the disabled vehicles would have to be cleared before the refugee millipede could again resume its slow, persistent move toward the promised land. Sometimes, they told us, the traffic jams were caused by army vehicles running out of fuel. Many of those burned-out vehicles we saw weren't the victims of air strikes at all. The Germans were ordered to destroy anything they abandoned. When a vehicle ran out of fuel, they pushed it off the road and set fire to it. Disposing of stalled vehicles stopped traffic; the heat and smoke from their disposal slowed it. Once we were stalled, it would take hours to get moving again.

We were only a few hours from crossing the Danube into Tolna province, very near our new home in the town of Bátaszék, when they learned that the bridge had been destroyed by two American bombers. The next nearest bridge was fifty-five kilometers to the north. Our journey of days was extended into weeks.

The weather was not so bad during the day, but the nights were cold. Dad had to disappear from time to time to escape the notice of German soldiers looking for able-bodied men to do manual labor for their army. I have a clear memory of how glad I was to see him when he returned from a two-day absence.

The worst part was the hunger. Once our food was gone, we had only occasional scraps. The bread Mom gave us was green, but we ate it anyway. Sometimes we begged at the houses we passed. Most people refused us. Other than the roofs over their heads, they had little or nothing themselves. My sisters and I cried a lot. We were always hungry, and there was constant noise, day and night, from the aeroplanes.

One day we arrived at a big river.

'Look, John! Look, Terry! It's the River Danube!' Mom rested baby Vera on her hip, as she pointed toward the water.

It was the first time in many days that I had seen her smile. The bridge had been bombed out here, too, but a ferry crossing had been set up. We waited in queue for hours and hours. Everywhere were the sounds of horses neighing, children crying, and the low rumble of adults making ordinary conversation among the mobile ruin of our lives.

I watched as wagon after wagon was loaded on the ferry. Most of the horses hesitated, and their owners coaxed them forward. It was necessary to blindfold some horses to lead them onto the ferry, but they panicked nonetheless as their hoofs hit the deck, making a loud, unfamiliar sound. We watched the ferry gate slam shut before us as the family in front of us positioned themselves in the last available space on the ferry. It was disappointing to see the ferry glide away without us, but now we were at the front of the queue, and before long we were boarding the next one. Mom and Dad stood beside us, and Terry and I sat on the wagon seat as the ferry took off, slowly crossing the river. Vera, usually a red, bawling bundle of protest, was lying on her back in the wagon bed, lulled into unusual silence by the gentle rocking motion of the ferry.

First ones on and first ones off, we were not too far away to watch the unhappy event as the last horse and wagon were being led from the ferry's deck. The horse, just as uneasy in debarking as it had been in embarking, suddenly panicked and charged backwards. The wagon it pulled broke through the rear gate and rolled into the river, taking the horse and all the young family's belongings with it. Everything had disappeared from view before onlookers had finished their first gasps of horrible surprise.

A woman stood on the bank screaming, and a man jumped frantically into the water. Mom whispered to Dad, who turned his back to the scene and urged our old horse forward. Crying and screams of grief and frustration had been a part of our everyday life for the past few weeks. It was easy to just turn away and look ahead as our wagon moved forward. Mom picked up Vera, holding her close to her breast. It was many years later, after I had children of my own, that Mom explained to me that there had been a baby in that wagon, and they had not been able to save it or retrieve its body.

Word passed down to us that there was a change in plans. Our promised houses in Bátaszék were still occupied by others. Temporary housing had been arranged in Zala, a community 150 kilometers west of our final destination.

We were 13,000 people riding in horse-drawn wagons or walking, dependent on the charity and goodwill of people we met along the way. A child takes for granted that you go where your parents go and life unfolds as it should. Crossing the Danube seemed to represent the end of the danger. We had stopped running away and now were traveling towards something. In my child's mind, the people who turned us away when we begged for food were the 'bad' people who did not like us. Yet there was always enough kindness to get us from one day to the next in the long march to Bátaszék.

5

Zala

In Zala, the older couple who took us in were very good to us. They had a large house, with a wide central hallway with rooms on both sides. They gave us a group of rooms at the back of the house to use as our own. My parents shared the farm work, and our hosts shared the vegetables, eggs, milk and meat produced on their farm. We were finally free of the straitjacket of hunger. My sisters and I resumed our jobs as children, clever angels one minute and naughty devils the next, taking delight in the world or blaming it for not granting our wishes.

The men would disappear to their day's work as the women began their day cleaning up from the family breakfast. Later, the women, too, would find their ways into the farmyard to feed animals or into the garden to harvest food for our meals. I was the only one among the children old enough to entertain myself outside my mother's sight.

Every morning, with my back to the sun, I watched the sky, waiting for the specks on the horizon to take shape as they approached, waiting for the distant rumble to become a deafening roar. As the bombers passed overhead, blotting out the sky, I was certain there must have been thousands and thousands of them. The people had a saying: 'The sky has measles.'

Throughout the day I could hear the distant sound of bombs exploding somewhere far, far away. In the afternoon, I would watch again as the sky filled with bombers returning west.

Sometimes when German fighters attempted to intercept the American bombers, I would see the battles overhead. They weren't like the sky battles you see in movies. There were no clever acrobatics or chasing games of catch-me-if-you-can. The fighter would appear suddenly, a short exchange of fire, then a thick, grey smoke billowed from one of them, followed by a parachute or two drifting towards the earth. The injured plane would dive and I would see a flash, followed a split second later by a huge bang. From beginning to end, less than a minute had elapsed.

Late one afternoon, when I was watching the bombers return from their day's work, a German fighter swooped from out of nowhere, rapidly disposing of an American bomber. The plane dove in the distance, but the billowing parachute sailed straight towards me, landing on the highway some twenty meters in front of me. It was the only time I was to see the face of one of the men we had watched ride their parachutes to earth. And it was the first time in my life I had seen a black man, as black as the richest farm land in the Carpathian Basin. The children stared in awe and fear. I was terrified. Before we could gather the courage to have a closer look, the police arrived, quickly taking him away, his pack still on his back and the white silk parachute gathered in a wad under his arm.

It was not too long after that I awoke one morning to find the town full of German soldiers. They camped their mobile kitchen about fifty meters from our house. We kids would hang around when they were cooking, hoping they would give us their leftovers. Sometimes they would give us a bit of something, but usually they just ran at us, shouting and waving their arms, as if they were running off stray dogs. Sometimes one of us would find our bum connected to the toe of a German boot. Our German allies were not touched by the sight of gangs of hungry children. They were no doubt too involved in the fragile and uncertain nature of their own existence.

One morning, I went out to play and saw groups of people, some walking, some half running through the snow. I followed the crowd about half a kilometer and pushed my way to the front through the forest of adult legs. There were bodies of German soldiers everywhere. Pools of bright red blood stained the white snow as far as I could see.

The dead I had seen on the march to Bátaszék, draped and strewn about the burned-out carcasses of tanks and trucks, had been at a distance, not really recognizable to my young boy's eyes as ever having been human. This, then, was my first sight of a dead person close up. I watched in horrid fascination as young people moved from body to body, pulling rings off fingers, pulling objects from pockets, taking for their own whatever they could find of value. I remember so clearly one body. One of his legs was half gone, and a teenager was bent over, pulling his watch from his arm. That severed leg may have worn a boot that had kicked me away from a pot of steaming food, yet, at that moment, I despised that teenager.

That must have been in December of 1944, when the Hungarian government collapsed and the new government declared war on Germany. The remaining Germans in the town began their retreat that day—not in orderly marching columns, but without leadership or direction. They were simply going home, most of them on foot, throwing away rifles and uniforms, trading or begging for civilian clothes. After a few days of disorderly retreat, there was sudden and absolute quiet. There was no one on the highway.

Within hours, I saw a few giant forms moving towards us along the open highway. They were Soviet tanks. Russian soldiers took the place of German soldiers, and in a few days, snowfall covered the splashed, red stains in the snow. It was as if the Germans had never been there.

I listened to the whispers of adults and learned that all the young women were hiding in cellars. I don't remember that anyone explained to me, and I don't remember being told that my mother's hiding place was a secret. But I remember knowing that it was important that the soldiers should not know where she was. I didn't realize until I was much older that everyone feared the Russians would claim the ancient victor's right to ravish the women. When a young woman needed to move about the town, she would wear the clothes of an old woman, smear dirt on her face and bend over as if her aging back would not allow her to walk erect.

The Russians set up their kitchen in the same block vacated by the retreating Germans. Their food was not as good as the Germans, but they were generous with it, always sharing with the hopeful kids who gathered. I guess I must have been a pitiful sight, small for my age, thin from going hungry so often, and shivering in the cold, with only a thin woolen shirt to warm me. A soldier slipped my arms into a boy's jacket, buttoned it closed in front and tucked some paper money and a pocket watch in the pocket. He gave me a smile and a pat, and I smiled back before I raced home to show off my good fortune.

Mom took one look and began jerking the jacket off me as quickly as she could move. It was alive with lice. I retrieved the treasures from the pocket before she stuffed the jacket into a pot of boiling water. She put me in the bath, scrubbed me with strong soap and picked my head clean of the creepy little invaders.

I don't know for certain if she kept the watch or sold it, but I remember her surprise when she unrolled the money to find two paper notes worth two thousand penzo each. It was February, 1945. We were soon to leave for Bátaszék, and the weeks of marching on empty stomachs from Bácska to Zala was still fresh in her mind. Mom used the money to buy food. Lots of food. She bought smoked hams, salamis and preserved foods of every kind. From the local farmers she bought plain flour for bread making and anything else that would keep well on a long journey. It was a story she liked to tell over and over in later years, the way we were saved from starvation by two paper notes tucked into a lice-infested gift package.

As the Russians prepared to resume their westward march towards Germany, they needed fresh supplies. They took our old grey horse, our wagon and the few chickens my mother had been raising. Throughout the town and surrounding farmland, they took every live animal they could find, the horses to haul their artillery and the pigs and chickens to eat. I remember one day watching the neighbouring farmer being confronted by four Russian soldiers. Their voices were angry and they were waving their rifles. I went off to play and forgot about it. That evening I heard my parents talking. The farmer had denied having a pig, and when the soldiers found it, they shot him on the spot.

The townspeople were absolutely terrified of the Russians. The worst thing was to be accused of being a capitalist. Capitalists were taken away, and no one ever saw them again. Despite their cruelties, the soldiers continued to show special kindness to children. After the stoic indifference of the German soldiers, the children welcomed the smiling faces of the Russian infantrymen.

One day I came upon our landlord being confronted by angry Russian soldiers. They were asking for wine from his cellar. They were already drunk and wanted more. They did not know he was deaf, and he had not learned to lip read Russian. The Russians became angrier and angrier at his silence. I knew they were swearing. Kids pick up words. One of the soldiers raised his pistol, aiming at the poor man's head.

'He doesn't understand you,' I blurted. 'He can't hear what you're saying.' I was pointing at my ear, trying to get them to understand. I was too young to understand the danger I was in.

I stepped forward, stood in front of the landlord, and explained to him what the soldiers had been saying. From then on, the old man was very good to me. I had saved his life, and he made sure that I didn't go hungry.

The Russians hung around the village for about two weeks. They must have been trying to establish some kind of defense, because all the able men they could find, including my father, were forced into service to dig trenches. When the Russians finally left, they took our men with them. Women and children undertook the hard labor of tending the planted fields. No one knew if we would ever see our men again. It was a hard time. There were no eggs, no milk and no meat. The Russians had taken everything.

It was three months before the men returned. Gaunt and weak from hard work and poor food, Dad came into the yard leading a horse he had found standing on the highway. It was a gift from heaven for a man who knew he was coming home to a farm stripped of its working animals. It was a fit horse but totally blind. Dad thought it must have been an army horse blinded by a canon flash. With the horse locked securely in the paddock and tears of happiness kissed away, Dad lay down to rest. It seemed to me that he did not get up for days, and a sickness of exhaustion consumed him for weeks.

Refuse of the dying war was everywhere. By the roadside there were piles of uniforms, weapons and munitions of every sort. They were an attractive nuisance for curious children. The older boys took powder out of bullets to make fireworks. I remember finding an explosive device of some sort that I thought was a grand toy. As I proudly walked about holding it by its tail-shaped handle, I was cautiously approached by a man who politely asked if he might hold it. I remember willingly handing it over. Once safely out of my hands, it was explained to me that had I dropped it, it could have blown up me and everyone around me.

It was April, 1945. The German occupation had ended, the Russian soldiers had gone home, and everyone had begun packing for the move to Tolna. The post-war Hungarian economy was drowning in chaos, and hyperinflation had taken hold of our national currency. If Mom had held onto those two paper notes two more months, they would have been worthless. It took a bag full of pengo to buy a single egg. No one wanted to accept paper money. The medium of exchange became jewelry, clothing, farm goods or anything else of value. But nonetheless the war was ended, and we were again on the way to our new homes in Hungary.

Four hundred of our Bukovina Székely families had been trapped with the Germans in Bácska and never made it into Hungary. Others had found their way to other places in Hungary, too tired or too unsure to make their way to our new 'promised land'. When we packed our few possessions onto our blind horse and faced towards our new homes in Bátaszék, our numbers were few. Of the 2,379 Székely families who had traveled by train from Bukovina to Bácska in 1941, only 245 arrived with us in Bátaszék on the 15th of May, 1945.

Our triumphant arrival in Bátaszék was a sad repetition of our 1941 migration to Bácska. The homes we were promised were not specially built for our arrival as they had been for our ancestors who settled in Bukovina 150 years before. Again, politicians were negotiating the currency of human lives. Hungary wanted to reclaim its own, to 'bring home' ethnic Hungarians who had lived for generations in Transylvania, Bukovina and Czechoslovakia. The problem of where to put them was resolved by disowning the centuries-old commitment to the Danube Swabians, a unique Hungarian people of Germanic origin, who had been recruited out of Germany, two and three centuries before, to establish farms to help grow the region's economy. Now the homes they had built and the land they had cultivated was no longer theirs by government decree. They were forced to evacuate their homes and migrate to Germany, their 'homeland'—a land now foreign, a place where many did not even understand the language. A very few were allowed to stay if they could prove their service in the Hungarian army.

Thus, our joy at having a home, at last, was coloured by the grief of our new neighbours whose families had migrated to Bátaszék more than 200 years before at the special invitation of the Austrian Imperial Council. Not all Swabs accepted their fate. Some hid in their wine cellars or in the surrounding forests and mountains and waited until it was safe to return. Most were caught and sent to join their neighbours in the forced move to Germany.

In Yugoslavia, Swabs who did not escape into Hungary were forced into concentration camps by the thousands. Their 200-year-old pact with Austria was ended, as they were no longer thought of as Hungarians or Yugoslavians, but were punished for their German ancestry and transported as the losers in the latest European struggle for territory. Among the Swabs who returned to Bátaszék—and their children and grandchildren—there still lingers some bitterness at the unfairness of their treatment.

6

Occupation in the Promised Land

Our journey to Bátaszék was not so dramatic and not so full of fear and dread as our escape from Bácska. It was spring 1945 when we arrived. The house allocated to us was still occupied, so we were again assigned to a family who shared their unit with us. They were very good to us. They even gave us kids money to buy lollies and my first taste of ice cream.

After the first Swab evacuation, there were still twenty-five of our families who did not have a place to live. They waited in temporary shelters while more Swab families were moved from their homes, loaded onto railway cattle wagons and transported to Germany. In this way 669 Swab families in Bátaszék lost their homes as Hungarian minorities from bordering countries were settled. I remember the nice woman who lived in the house next to ours and how sad I felt for her the day she had to leave. I had heard that the Swabs were returning home, the way my family had returned home. But she wasn't happy about it, and I didn't understand why she had to go if she didn't want to.

Each of our Bukovina Székely families was given a house and land according to the size of the family. All land had been measured and pegged with the name of the new owner. It included vineyards, some very good land and some not-so-good land. Almost all new owners had scattered bits of land in three or four different locations, up to three kilometers from the house. My parents attended government-sponsored evening classes to learn how to look after the grapes, how and when to prune the vines, spray for disease and harvest in anticipation of winemaking.

In addition to a house for our family, there was a small, two-room farm house in our vineyard that was still occupied by a man in his early sixties, who was waiting to be called for his transport to Germany. He was there for about three months, and I liked spending time with him. He took the time to entertain a small boy, telling great stories and making music with the trumpet that he had played as a member of the local marching band before the war. When he left, he gave the trumpet to me. I lost it, but sometimes I think Mom hid it or gave it away. I was very good at making a very loud sound but not so skillful at making music.

Our new home was big and comfortable with a big backyard. The government gave us money and basic food stuffs, like the plain flour my mother used to make her bread, as well as corn to feed the animals. It was a loan, not a gift.

It wasn't until I was grown and living on another continent that I read that families who had migrated to Bátaszék from the north had had quite a different experience from ours. With three months to plan for their move and, typically, an allotment of four railway wagons per family, they arrived with ploughs, farm implements, furniture, clothing, family treasures, horses and sometimes other farm animals. I guess my parents were too grateful for the end of the deprivation of war and running away from war to compare themselves to our more fortunate neighbours. I never heard them mention it.

My mother said it was very hard work to start again with so little. We arrived with our blind horse and our wagon, which was just about worn out after our long journey. We were issued farm tools, including a plough. Farmers were expected to help each other and share farm implements. My memory is that it worked well, especially among relatives. My father's large family created for us a strong, close-knit community who chipped in to help each other.

Our happiness in our spacious, new home was short lived. In order to induce the ethnic Hungarians from Czechoslovakia to voluntarily resettle within the postwar borders of Hungary, the government had guaranteed them that they would have homes as large and accommodating as the ones they were leaving behind. A group of these Upperlanders, as we called the Czech Hungarians, were settled in Bátaszék, and one family was very unhappy with their new home. It was far smaller than the one they had left behind in Czechoslovakia, they said, and they were vocal and persistent in their protest.

Years later I would hear Mom say over and over, 'He drank away our home.' If the story I was later told is accurate, it was more that he was swindled while in an accommodating alcoholic fog. It was never clear to me that Dad even knew what he had done.

As the story goes, the governing committee invited Dad for a drink or two, and when he was sufficiently bereft of sober judgment, convinced him to sign a document legally transferring our spacious home to a Czech Hungarian family in exchange for a small, two-bedroom house. Mom went to the committee and complained, but she only succeeded in having waved in her face the legal document signed by Dad. The committee had solved their immediate problem, a family of Upperlanders were granted the home they had been promised, and the affection between my parents had suffered another blow. More than any other sin of his drinking, I think this one thing caused the greatest and most lasting bitterness.

Mom said the first two or three years in Bátaszék were more difficult than they thought they would be. There were very good harvests of wheat, corn, grapes and other crops, but we still had to pay taxes on our house and land and make payments on the start-up loan. Mom and Dad were also trying to buy new farm tools, cattle, chickens, pigs and other investments in our farm's future. By the time loan payments, taxes and other farming expenses were paid, very little was left for feeding and clothing the family until the next year's harvest. There were many days that we ate very little; some days we went without. I was not a courageous little man about the deprivation. I was resentful. Unaware how many others were suffering just as we did, I blamed my parents for not having the things I imagined other people had.

My parents had long looked forward to this freedom, but it was a short-lived illusion. Our liberation from German occupation by the Russians was, in fact, a Russian occupation. By 1949, the new direction was very clear. Dominated by our Russian 'liberators', our new government adopted a strong anti-capitalist stance. Anyone who did well and began to accumulate a little money was accused of being supporters of the capitalist system. People with such 'American ideas' were stripped of their property and assets and sometimes imprisoned, too. People were frightened that their neighbours would dob them in for having extra animals or appearing more prosperous than others in the community. Many tried to hide their assets, not declaring them for taxation. These people always went to jail, and some of them never returned home.

The government appointed special tax collectors with unlimited powers. Frightening stories began to circulate. Farmers who didn't pay the full amount of their tax levy were subject to merciless seizures of personal property. The tax collectors took the horses, cows and whatever else they could put their hands on. Delinquent taxpayers with no remaining assets to be seized were jailed for two to three years, and their families sank into poverty with no working animals and no men in their families to work their land.

In the early 1950s, in the midst of this tense and hostile economic environment, my father was visiting one of his sisters on a special holiday. I think they had had a couple of glasses of wine when the tax collectors turned up. Her kids were crying, her husband wasn't home, and with a few glasses of courage under his belt, my father told them it was a public holiday so they should just piss off because the man of the house was not at home. They left, but the matter was far from settled.

In the evening, two policemen came to our house and arrested my father. We were in the middle of the wheat harvest. Mom cried because there was no one to help us with the wheat harvest. Everyone in Dad's family had their own harvests to tend. I was the only boy in the family, so at twelve years of age, I told my mother I could do it. I had never handled the scythe before and had to learn how to swing it, how to achieve a rhythm and when and how to sharpen the blade. My farm work had to be done early in the morning and after school each day. I couldn't just ditch school until harvest was over; attending school was compulsory. I dropped exhausted into bed each night and woke stiff and in pain each morning. It was hard labour over the course of a week. Mom cried every evening, moaning that she must be cursed to have a husband in jail and a young son doing men's work. My older half sister, Appolonia, was living with us then, and she and my mother pitched in, and the three of us finished the harvest, including picking the corn and the grapes. By the time winemaking was in progress, my father was out of jail. His six-month sentence had been reduced to three months with the promise that he would never again be disrespectful to the tax collectors.

Mom was very proud of me, and I felt very grown up being called upon to do a man's job and finding that I could do it. But my young body had not been ready for the ordeal. My back was never again strong, and years later I was diagnosed with curvature of the spine.

After we settled in Bátaszék, things were better. Well, some things anyway. We never had money, but there was always food. During the war food had been scarce, and before Dad joined the collective farm, the tax collectors kept us too poor to have decent food. Mom would put plain flour in the fry pan with a little lard and heat it until it went brown. Sometimes we ate it with bread, sometimes with a little corn flour to dip into it. But after we joined the collective and no longer had to pay high taxes, Mom began to cook the best meals. Her donuts were fantastic and her Hungarian goulash the best. Years later when she came to Australia for a visit, she stayed for three months and cooked every day. The neighbours took to coming over in the evenings to see what she was cooking. She would give samples of her cooking, and she taught many of our neighbours how to make her special cabbage rolls.

7

Time To Be a Kid

Even when times were hard, our parents found ways for us to be kids, sometimes re-creating the traditions that they remembered from their own childhoods. For me, the 6th of December, Saint Nicholas Day, was the best day of the year to be a kid. On that evening, my sisters and I would put our boots or shoes outside our bedroom doors. If I had been a good boy, I could expect to find lollies in my shoes the next morning; if not, I would get sticks. I learned early that it was important to be a good boy, at least the couple of days before Saint Nicholas Day.

The old Swab man who had lived in the small house by our winery spent hours entertaining me with stories—stories of his childhood, stories from history, scary stories and stories of magic. I loved the scary stories most of all. It was Christmas of 1947 when I determined to weave a magic spell of my own from one of these stories.

I had to build a three-legged chair, starting work on the 6th of December. But there were very strict conditions to it. The chair had to be built of wood only, no other materials. I had to have it completed not sooner and not later than the 24th of December, and I had to work on it every day, no matter how little. On Christmas Eve, I was to attend midnight mass and bring with me to the church a stick and my three-legged chair. When the church clock struck the first sound of the twelve o'clock chime, I was to run to the nearest road crossing, which represents the cross, place the chair in the middle of the crossing and sit on it. With the stick, I was to draw a circle around me. Within this magic circle, nothing could harm me. I was particularly interested in guarding myself from being harmed by the magic genie who would appear as I sat there. The genie would offer me three bribes to coax me out of my circle of protection. No matter how good his bribes sounded, I was not to take any of it, because once I stepped outside the circle, very bad things would happen to me. If I passed the test of the three bribes, the genie would give me anything I wanted. The hard part would be that I would have to keep the genie busy all the time. As soon as he got one thing for me, I would have to immediately find something else for him to do for me.

'There is only one way to get rid of the genie,' the old man had told me.

'How?' I had asked.

'I don't know,' he replied, 'that's something you'll have to figure out for yourself.'

I thought about all that and decided I was up to the challenge. By the time I got everything I wanted, I thought, the genie would be sick of me. I would have all the money, ice creams, chocolates and lollies, and the genie would just go away, tired of working for me. I had it all figured out. I knew I could beat the genie.

As soon as the 6th of December came, I started on my three-legged chair. Every day after school, I would tell Mom that I was going to clean the stable. And every day, I would work on my chair, hiding it beneath a pile of straw when it was time to go back to the house. I made sure I stuck to the rules. There were no nails, only wooden pegs to hold it together.

My mother and father always went to the midnight mass on Christmas Eve. It was my habit to pretend that I was asleep when I heard them getting ready to go. But not this time. When it was time to go, I ran to the stable to fetch my chair.

'What's that?' my father asked.

'It's a chair,' I answered. 'I made it myself.'

'And what are you going to do with it?' he asked.

'I'm going to sit in it,' I answered. 'The church is always full and we kids have to stand because grownups want all the seats. So I made my own chair to sit on.'

He let out a great laugh. 'As long as you carry it,' he said.

We lived about a kilometer from the church. It was snowing heavily, and my arms grew tired from carrying the chair. Just as I was thinking I couldn't carry that chair another step, the church came into view. We looked like snow men as we mounted the church steps. We stomped and shook and brushed the snow from our clothes before entering the church. Dad smiled at me as I placed my chair just inside the door, and he and Mom made their way to an empty pew. The church soon filled up. I was ready. There was a main crossing about 20 meters from where I sat.

The other people in the church were singing Christmas songs, but not me. I was watching the snow fall heavier and heavier as I waited for the church bell to chime at midnight. By now, each time I looked out the door, I could hardly see the street light. The snow on the road was at least 300 millimeters deep. I waited and waited, and when the bell finally chimed, I jumped with a start, picked up my chair and ran as fast as I could through the drifting snow. I made it to the crossing and set my chair where I imagined the exact middle to be. I sat down with great satisfaction, then remembered that I had forgotten to bring the stick. It was still standing in the corner of the stable where I had propped it next to my chair.

What a dilemma I now faced. I knew that I had to stay on the chair, no matter what, so I reached with my right arm as far as I could, rotating with the chair to draw a circle in the snow. It was a splendid circle. I was sitting there admiring my work when the street light went out. I was now in complete darkness. I couldn't see my hands. I wasn't scared because I knew this was the first test to see how tough I am. I sat confidently on the chair, waiting for the next test.

Before long, I began to feel very cold and started to think it might be a better idea to call the whole thing off. It was freezing and the snow had begun to fall again. I was just about to stand up and walk away when I heard a noise—not too far away and coming closer and closer. It was the genie! I knew that I must stay in my chair no matter what happened. The sounds were very close now, and as the church door opened, light from the church outlined two monster shapes moving towards me. I could hear heavy breathing.

'Don't move, don't move,' I kept telling myself. 'Don't move, no matter what happens.'

By now, I was shaking and my teeth were chattering. 'It's just the freezing cold,' I told myself, but I tucked my head down so that I couldn't see the monsters. When I couldn't stand another minute without knowing, I opened my eyes. There before me were two horse heads, steam blowing from their nostrils.

'Who's there?' I heard a voice calling.

'Me,' I answered weakly.

'Me who?' the voice demanded. I recognized the voice. It was the voice of Uncle Frank, my father's younger brother. I knew it was the genie playing tricks on me, and I was determined not to give up.

'Is that you?' came Uncle Frank's voice.

'Yes, it is me,' I answered defiantly.

'What the bloody hell are you doing there? Are you gone crazy?'

'No, I'm not.' I was brave again in the knowledge that I was staring down the genie and I would win. I shouted back, 'I know that you are only playing tricks on me, and I'm not going to move.'

The genie began swearing at me with Uncle Frank's voice and threatened to ring my neck if I didn't get out of the way. Suddenly he stopped shouting and cursing and began pleading with me to get out of the way.

'If this is Uncle Frank, why is he not going around me?' I asked myself. There was plenty of room to do that.

'Uncle Frank, you are not real,' I shouted at the genie.

'What did you say? I'm not real?' The genie who looked exactly like Uncle Frank got off his wagon seat and started towards me. 'You'd better move or I'll kick your ass,' he said.

'You can't do that, I have a ring around me!'

The words formed in my throat but half of them never made it out before he had picked me up by the collar of my coat and set me down at the side of the road. He kicked the chair away, got back on his wagon and drove on.

I was in a state of shock. The mass was finished and people were coming out of the church. I ran back to the church and forgot all about the chair.

On the way home, my father noticed my empty arms. 'Where's your chair?' he asked.

'Oh, one leg broke off so I threw it away,' I answered.

Even now, I'm thinking maybe it didn't work because I broke the rules. *I forgot the stick,* so the ring around me wasn't big enough. At first I thought I would try it again, but I began to worry about what would happen if I couldn't keep the genie busy after I had everything I wanted. What if I never figured out how to send him away? So I chickened out.

Speaking of chickens, I had one other magical adventure. It was another of the old man's stories, and I determined to carry it out the spring following my close call with the genie who sounded like Uncle Frank.

In spring my mother would buy forty or fifty old chickens from the hatchery. By old, I mean they were too old to be sold as chicks and usually in poor condition. She would lose a dozen or so during the first few weeks, but on a diet of milled corn soaked in water and the careful attention of my mother, by early summer we would have fresh chickens to eat and some would start to lay eggs. With a new batch of spring chickens, I began to carry out the magic spell, just the way the old man had told it to me.

For this one, I had to have the first egg laid by a black hen after mating with a black rooster. So from among Mom's spring chickens, I chose a black hen and a black rooster. To keep them out of the cooking pot, I convinced Mom that these were 'my two favourite chickens'. To her it made no difference, so it never became an issue. Every day, when I came home from school, I checked that everything was going according to plan. The rooster and the hen were growing nicely. There were only two roosters in the flock, an old rooster from the year before and my rooster, the newcomer. When they started to fight, one of them had to go into the pot. Since the black one was 'my favourite', Mom sacrificed the old rooster, leaving mine the only male in the chicken community.

One day I noticed the young rooster was beginning to mate with the older chickens. It was the signal for me to spend more time in the backyard so I wouldn't miss anything. I didn't have to wait long. Within a few days I saw the black rooster and the black hen mating. Now I had to come up with a very good story to convince my mother that the hen should be separated from the rest.

Mom had a small area fenced off for sick or injured animals, so I caught the hen and pulled some feathers from her head. I placed her in the 'hospital' pen and told Mom that the rest of the chickens were attacking her. Mom put me in charge of my favourite hen's recovery. She warned that it was up to me to make sure that it got fed and watered every day, or come Sunday it would be in the pot for lunch. I looked after my hen and didn't have to wait long. Three days later, I found an egg about the size of a pigeon egg. The old man had told me the first egg would be smaller than normal. Everything was going just as he instructed.

Now I was ready to proceed to the next step. I had to keep the egg under my arm until it hatched. When it hatched, there would be a little devil, but I was not to worry because nobody else would see him and nobody else would hear him but me. The little devil would grant me three wishes, and, unlike the genie, he would then disappear. I could only remove the egg from under my arm for very short periods of time—only to get washed and dressed or undressed. I would have to hold it even when I was in bed.

The first day, I held my arm rigid until I reached school, where I took several lengths of sticky tape and fixed the egg to my underarm. It worked for a few hours, but then body oil or perspiration began to affect the mucilage, and the tape detached. I stuck it back, but it failed to hold again and again. I came so near to dropping it that I knew I had to come up with a better idea. And I did. When I got home from school, I tore up one of my old shirts and made a little sack just big enough to hold the egg, attached two strips and wrapped it around my shoulder. It was perfect. I had nearly all my freedom back to do my chores and I could stop pretending that I had a sore arm.

The old man hadn't told me how long it would take for an egg to hatch. As I waited, I dreamed about my three wishes. I knew my first wish was plenty of money. The other two wishes I wasn't sure. I was only eight years old, but I had figured out that I needed money to buy things.

I don't remember how many days I had been coddling my egg, waiting for it to hatch, when the unthinkable happened. I awoke one morning to a wet, gooey sensation in my armpit. I lifted my arm to look and was shocked wide awake by the sight of bits of shell, yolk and white stuck to my underarm. I held back the tears and determined that I would try again the next spring. But I didn't. By the time another summer, autumn and winter had come and gone, I had lost interest in the practice of magic.

8

School Days

Schools throughout Hungary had been closed for at least four years because of the war. When I started school in 1946, I had missed two years of education, but others had missed more. In the traditional manner, boys and girls attended separate schools. The boys in my first grade class were as young as six and as old as thirteen. We were all seeking a normalcy, a catching up from those lost years. The school building was in a terrible state of disrepair, and for the first few months, our lessons were given over the sounds of saws and hammers as repairs were made.

My education was no different from the rest. I was very lucky, though, that I had a very good memory, because there was never time for homework or play after school. Everyone had to contribute to keep the farm going, and I had chores every day. I cleaned the stable and the pigs' pen, fed the chickens and ducks, and whatever other jobs my mom and dad found for me. Our school holidays occurred at harvest time, which meant that there were no holidays for me. Sunday was our day of rest, and the only day we were allowed to be just kids. I had to go to church, but after that my cousins and I attended the matinee at the movies. That was the only time we saw girls our own age.

In grade one, it was arranged for us to learn a foreign language. On offer were German and French. But by the time I was to go for the first lesson, they changed it. Only one language was offered: Russian became compulsory for everyone. Learning to speak their language was not the only practical subject our Communist benefactors taught us. We were trained to fight capitalism within our community and to defend ourselves against attack from the outside by the English or Americans or other capitalist countries. Beginning at twelve years of age, we were all taught how to use guns in the event of a Capitalist invasion.

Our education was compulsory through eight years of school. When I finished grade five, I was invited to join a special class who would complete the work of grades six and seven in one school year. When we assembled there were fifteen boys and fifteen girls, our first experience with boys and girls together in a class. On the first day, we had to listen to the principals from the girls' and boys' schools. We were told that we were picked because our teachers were sure that we could do two years of education in one year. And for us, there would be no school holidays. We would stay in class two hours longer every day; and on Saturdays, instead of being finished at one o'clock in the afternoon, we would finish at two and sometimes three o'clock.

It was hard work but it was my best time in school. We became very close to each other. Everybody helped everybody. We always knew that we had something to prove. Whatever we did, we did it together, and together we all hated our Russian class.

One day the Russian teacher sat down, then jumped up immediately, shouting, 'Who did it?'

I didn't know what he was talking about. He was fuming with anger and repeatedly demanded to know who had done it. When no one came forward, he stormed out of the classroom. As soon as he was out of ear shot, the room buzzed with naughty excitement. Those who knew delightedly shared their knowledge with those who didn't. One of my mates had put a few open baby pins on the teacher's chair, so that they all stuck in his bottom when he sat down. We each solemnly pledged that we would not tell.

Before long, the Russian teacher, the principal and two other teachers entered our classroom. Our teacher assured us that if we would tell who it was, we wouldn't be punished. It didn't work; we maintained our loyal silence. Obviously agitated, the principal announced that we would be locked in our classroom until the perpetrator came forward or one of us told who it was. The four of them left the classroom and locked the door behind them. It was not long before one of the teachers appeared at the door and called the name of a student, who was ordered to follow him to the principal's office. One by one, each of us was called for a private interview with the principal, and one by one, each was offered a bribe of secrecy, promised that if we would tell, it would be a secret and no one would ever find out. That didn't work either. We proudly held fast in our common promise. When it got dark, they let us go home. I'm certain, to this day, no one outside our group ever learned the truth. So in that one year, we became more than friends.

Out of our group of thirty, only two didn't complete the year, because their families moved out of town. At year's end, we were all awarded a certificate for our achievements. Then the girls went back to the girls' school, and we boys started year eight in the boys' school.

When I finished year eight, my marks were above average. All my teachers told me to go to high school. The high school was about thirty kilometers away. That meant I would have to travel by train. It was a one-hour journey each way. Despite the support and encouragement of my teachers, my father would not listen to what they had to say. 'I need him on the farm,' he would say when another teacher would visit to try to convince him. And that was that. Upon graduation from primary school, I became a farm hand instead of a high school student.

A couple of years later, when Dad and most of the other farmers gave into the coercion to join the collective farm, we found that there were more benefits to our membership than just getting the tax collectors off our backs. It also meant that my family didn't need me all the time just to keep the farm working and viable. It was too late for me to start high school, but I was soon to find another opportunity.

I think it was late November, when I was fourteen, that my mother and I visited my grandmother and her youngest sister, my Auntie Sabina. There was a big coal mine nearby and adjoining it a school of mines. The school promised adult pay for students who passed their exams. When I learned about this, I saw it as my chance to escape the farm and do something else with my life. I convinced my mother that I wouldn't be needed on the farm with winter coming on, and my income would help the family more than my labour. With her blessing, I enrolled in the Komlo School of Mines. I only had to bring my own underwear. Everything else was supplied—uniforms, toiletries, books and all learning materials.

It was run like a military school, very strict with academic classes, physical education and instruction in health and well-being. The food and accommodation were very good. There were two years in the classroom and one year of practical training in the coal mine.

Auntie Sabina lived near the school, and my grandmother (my mother's mother) lived with her. During school holidays, I would often go to stay with them. I looked forward to my visits because they were great cooks, and they treated me as visiting royalty, with great feasts of my favourite foods.

The certification I earned was half way between miner and mining engineer. I suppose it would have been considered a sort of middle management. I finished with honours and decided to go back home for a long break to decide what to do next, whether to push forward into a mine-engineering course or pursue some other direction. It was the winter of 1955. I was seventeen years old.

9

Communist Youth Leader

Eventually everyone, including my family, joined the collective farm. The Communists used a series of tactics to make it appear to be a free choice. The most effective were land swaps, where a farmer's good land would be taken away and in exchange he would get land that needed development or even land that could never be developed into profitable farmland. Added to that were taxes in the form of grain levies that were more than the farm could produce.

Once Dad had joined the collective farm, things became much better for him. He no longer had to worry about the high land taxes that made it impossible for an independent farmer to survive, and his workload was lighter and easier to manage.

I was home from the mining school in 1956 when the collective farm chairman called in to visit with my father. When Dad introduced me as his son returned from school, the chairman asked me if I would like to help my father for a few weeks. Dad's winter job was to feed and groom eighteen horses and to clean the stables. It was snowing heavy outside and cold. I thought of the nice, warm stables and agreed. Weeks went into months, and the chairman often stopped in for a chat. We had become pretty good friends, and one day he asked if I would organize and set up a club for the youth of the collective farm, both boys and girls. I accepted the job and found I had a generous budget.

I went to the city and bought table-tennis tables and other game equipment, and also a radio for music. I organized meetings to see what they wanted to do on Sundays and in their spare time. The chairman was a very good man; everyone liked him. He didn't manage with threats but with wise understanding.

'This is the world we live in,' he told me. 'Let's make the best of it.'

I didn't agree with most of the Communist regime and its dogma, but we all learned to go along with it. Otherwise we would finish up in special camps or in jail. I had a bitter memory of my father going to jail for speaking his mind. We all had to be very careful what we said, especially in front of young children, because kids talk at school and spies were everywhere. Nobody trusted anybody; nobody dared to criticize the government for any wrongdoing. So everything became a big lie, and we learned to put up with it.

So I stayed on the collective farm, and I was appointed Secretary of Youth. It was a good time for my family. The morale of the farmers was good, and the work I was assigned was challenging and enjoyable. I was sent to lots of training seminars, some politically oriented and some to teach organizing skills.

In September of that year, I was called to the manager's office and he asked if I would like to go to a three-week leadership course. I accepted, leaving Bátaszék by train the 18th of September, 1956.

I changed trains once, in Budapest. The training was held at Kismaros in an army training camp. The food and accommodation were outstanding: nothing but the best of everything. The course was all about politics and government policies. I was shocked that the teachers, most of whom were high-ranking army officers, openly criticized our Communist leaders. I remember thinking it was a trick to see if any of us would agree with their dangerous opinions. Perhaps others thought as I did, and we all kept our mouths shut.

On the 23rd of October, about seven o'clock in the morning, I caught the train to go back home.

10

A Revolution

The train ride to Budapest lasted about an hour. It was early when I arrived and I had time before I had to catch the train to Bátaszék. It was a nice day, so I decided to go sightseeing. I caught the tram to the zoo, spent some time there, then went to the amusement park and tried a few rides. When I thought it was time to go to the southbound railway station to catch the train home, I wasn't sure which tram to catch, so I got on the first one that came. As it worked out, it wasn't the right one, and I got lost. I asked for directions from an old lady who wasn't quite sure, so I asked some high school kids who were passing by.

'Come along with us,' one of the girls said. 'We'll show you which tram to catch.' I walked some distance with them and I think they forgot about me. When they got on a tram, I followed. The tram was full of students going to some protest march. I asked again for help finding my way.

'Where are you from?' the young man asked.

'Bátaszék', I answered.

'Never heard of it,' he responded.

He promised that when the march finished, he would take me to the southbound railway station. It was close to where he lived, he said. I got off when the protestors got off, keeping in my sights the student who promised to show me the way to the train station. We joined a flow of hundreds of students moving down the street, singing and shouting demands for better conditions.

'Where are we going?' I asked.

'To the radio station' was the answer.

I followed the young man who was to help me find my way as the crowd grew larger and larger. One minute there was a festive atmosphere, with singing and shouting; a few minutes later, there were bursts of gunfire, and panic broke out all around me. Everyone was pushing and shoving, and suddenly I was running for my life. The boy who promised to show me how to get to the railway station was limping. In the panic, someone had kicked him. The gunfire sounded closer and closer. I followed him into a side street, my heart throbbing fiercely. The sounds of gunfire and panic began to fade, and we slowed our pace, trying to hide our fear with frozen smiles. We must have been walking about ten minutes, when we boarded a passing tram. I followed him when he hopped off and onto another. We rode for another few minutes, and then he nudged my shoulder.

'Get off here,' he told me. 'That way,' he said, pointing towards a nearby street sign. 'You'll see the station when you get to the corner.'

I stepped off the tram and waved in thanks as it pulled away. That was the last time I saw him.

I had a nervous hour's wait until I boarded the train. It was around two o'clock in the morning when I finally arrived home. By the next day, news of the student demonstration in Budapest had reached Bátaszék. And it was not long before everyone realized that talking about it could be very dangerous. Throughout Hungary, a Russian military presence became evident. Even our small town was full of spies and informers. We all kept our mouths shut and hoped that the Russians would take their army back home. Farmers worked their land as usual, everyone tried to look normal, to pretend nothing had happened. But it was being talked about in whispers among family members and close friends. And by now, everyone was calling it a revolution, and I had been an eyewitness, something that I had not yet told anyone.

A week or so later, my best friend Dezso and I took a walk on the main street. I had finally mustered the courage to tell him what had happened to me in Budapest. Several of our friends joined us as we walked, until there were six or seven of us. We had all been bursting to talk about it, and now all we could talk about was revolution. We walked and talked until it was nearly dark.

We had just decided to head home, trying to beat the dark, when military vehicles appeared, seemingly out of nowhere, and halted at the intersection where we were standing. There were trucks carrying about sixty or seventy men, two Russian T54 tanks and two armored vehicles. We were relieved to see that it was a Hungarian army unit, coming from the direction of Budapest. They were all young kids, like us, except for the officer, who was a bit older, maybe in his thirties.

He asked us if we knew of any Russian soldiers about. They were not seeking them out but trying to avoid a confrontation. Dez told them not to go to Baja because there was a Russian base there. Then someone else suggested they go south, towards Mahacs or Pecs.

'Come with us,' a bloke called from a truck. He was joined by others, shouting and urging us to join them.

'Support the revolution!'

'It's your duty!'

'There's plenty of room for all of you,' the officer said.

We looked at one another. Only one moment's hesitation. Dez and I and two of our friends climbed aboard as the officer handed each of us a loaded machine gun, pointing towards the safety as he placed it in our hands. The Russians had taught us how to use these weapons against the capitalists, and now we would be turning our guns on them. As the trucks pulled away, we saw our other friends hurrying away into the night. Now it was official. I had joined the revolution—and this time it was no accident.

It was past midnight when our convoy arrived in Bata, a few kilometers south of Bátaszék. The officer in charge found someone to open the town hall for us, where we spent the night.

I woke to the deafening sound of a nearby gunshot. Someone had shot himself in the foot with his rifle. It wasn't bad; the bullet only grazed his foot. As our convoy resumed its journey, we were in good humour, still enjoying the joke of our mate nearly shooting off his toe. But as the day wore on, I began to experience the first flashes of fear, and I could see it in the faces of the others. Every time an aeroplane circled overhead, we stopped and took cover at the side of the road. This was for real; it was not a game.

The plan had been to go to the city of Pecs, but we were running low on fuel. They diverted the convoy into the city of Mohacs, where we filled up all the vehicles, then continued on towards Pecs. Twice we stopped and drove into the forest to hide when we received reports that the Russians were coming our way. When nothing happened, we continued our journey. We must have been very close to Pecs when a unit smaller than ours stopped us. I don't know what was said, but we turned around and went back the way we had come. About half way to Mohacs, we turned off the highway onto a dirt road. We had not gone far when we were ordered to abandon our vehicles and take cover. If the enemy appeared, our officer ordered us to fire to kill. We laid low for a couple of hours, growing stiff and tense, our fingers ready at the trigger. But nothing happened. It got dark, and we climbed back onto the covered trucks and slept. I remember that I slept good. I think we all were very tired. The next morning when they were handing out canned food for our breakfast, I noticed that some of the officers had changed their uniforms for civilian clothes.

After we had eaten and done our toiletries, they called us together for a meeting. They heard some bad news, they told us, about something that happened close to Komlo, a mining town not too far away. They told us all to go home, to get rid of our weapons and munitions and say nothing to anyone. In an odd way, it was good news for most of us. We were hungry and tired and yearned for the comforts of our homes. We left the tanks hidden in the shrubs, made our way to the highway and began the long walk home.

We four Bátaszék revolutionaries arrived home in the night. We stopped at the edge of town, where a small bridge spanned a narrow canal full of water. It was there we threw our rifles, machine guns and hand grenades into the deep, muddy water. I'm sure they are still at the mud bottom of that canal.

It was not so unusual that I would disappear for a few days. Sometimes I would go off with my friends or away on business for the Youth Committee. So when I returned home, I didn't expect questions. Usually, no one talked about politics, even with family. If you knew nothing, there was nothing to confess or report. I must have had a funny look on my face when I came in.

'Are you alright?' Mom asked.

I told my parents everything. They warned me not to say a word to anybody. I think each of my friends were scared that one of the others might talk. The secret police were everywhere. The local Communists seemed keen to play a part in the punishment of anyone who had participated, no matter how small their contribution. They wanted to set examples.

We feared Russian retribution. When World War II ended, the Americans and English emptied their prisoner-of-war camps; their former enemies were simply sent home. The Russians were not so forgiving. My cousin's husband, who had been conscripted by the Hungarian government to fight with the Germans against the Russians, returned home in 1954. Blinded in combat, he had been held in a Russian prison camp since the early days of World War II. And when he finally returned home, he was harassed by the Secret Police, treated as an enemy of the state. Years later, in 1974, my mother wrote me that a few more men had come home that year.

It was the 13th of January, 1957, when Dez told me he had heard the secret police were after us. We had no way of checking out the rumour to find out if it was true. We were taking no chances, and we ran. For us, the revolution was over. We had been revolutionaries for only three days.

11

Again a Refugee

I said goodbye to my mother on the 14th day of January, 1957. Staying was too dangerous, we thought, because of the stories that were circulating about people being shot or captured and tortured in jails. Neither of us thought that I would be leaving for good—just until things quieted down. I couldn't take anything with me for fear the police would suspect, so when I left, on the day of my nineteenth birthday, all I took was my ID card, a little money and the clothes I was wearing.

Dez and I were not the only ones making a run for it. When we boarded the bus in Bataszék at four o'clock in the afternoon, there were six of us, all veterans of the aborted foray to Pecs. A whisper here and a whisper there, and we soon learned there were at least thirty others on the bus who had the same idea. The western border into Austria had been closed. We had no choice but to attempt a crossing of the southern border into Yugoslavia. We had been traveling for about two hours when the bus came to a halt about a kilometer from the border. Our escape was an open secret. Even the bus driver knew. He told us where the guard towers were and wished us all luck.

The group of us took off towards the border. We agreed to walk separately in pairs. If one or two of us got caught, the others could continue unnoticed while the guards busied themselves with their new prisoners. It was getting dark and snow had begun to fall. Before long, we were making our way in the dark, unable to see more than three centimeters ahead in the falling snow.

The heavy snowfall protected us, hiding our presence even from each other. Dez and I walked together holding hands; it was so dark that we couldn't see each other. The snow was up to my knees, and sometimes we fell into drifts up to our necks. Suddenly the snowfall eased and we could see light about 100 meters in front of us.

We were walking towards the light, when we heard a terrifying noise, a booming voice saying, 'Stoy!'

We knew that was the Russian word for stop. We stopped where we stood, and my heart stopped, too. My teeth were chattering from cold and fear.

'Bloody Russians,' I said to Dez.

We quickly pushed our hands into the air, hoping they would not shoot us without even bothering to come closer. As they neared, I couldn't believe my eyes.

'They're not Russians!' I almost shouted from relief.

We didn't know that *stoy* meant the same thing in the Yugoslavian language.

One of the border guards came forward and searched our back and pockets, then told us we could put our hands down. Others emerged from the darkness, each in turn searched and herded into a group. We were ordered to follow one of the guards; another walked behind us. They had torches to light the way. There was no chance of being lost from sight now.

We walked about a kilometer to a square, concrete-block building. It was the community jail. We were in the border town of Belamanastir. They locked us up, about fourteen or fifteen of us, behind bars in one cell. I don't know what happened to the others who were on our bus. Maybe the Russians got them. Maybe they got lost and went the wrong way. Maybe they just decided they'd go back home and take their chances.

We talked to quiet our fear, to firm our resolve and to come to terms with what we were doing. I watched Dez doze off in the middle of a sentence, and then I must have slipped into sleep, too.

We were awake at daylight when they came to get us. Someone asked a guard where we were going.

'To Osijek,' he replied abruptly.

Two armed guards ordered the lot of us to climb into an open truck bed. We sat directly on the cold metal bottom of the truck. I got a lucky seat between two people, so the freezing cold air didn't get to me so bad. We were near frozen by the time we arrived.

I remember looking at the clock in the police station. It was close to midday. We had had nothing to eat or drink since leaving home. I remember a man asking for a glass of water for his young son.

'Go back to Hungary if your boy wants a drink of water,' the policeman replied in very good Hungarian. He said it quietly, as if he had said nothing more than, 'Have a nice day.' His eyes looked through us, as if we were not there at all.

They took our identification papers, and then, one by one, they interviewed us and locked us in cells. By now, there were fifty or sixty of us, including women and children of all ages, but still nothing to drink or eat. It was nearly three o'clock in the afternoon. Someone asked a guard if we could have something to eat.

'After you get to the camp,' he answered.

It was about four o'clock and still freezing outside when they told us to get back on the truck. About half an hour's drive, we arrived at a large farm house. At last, we would be warm. But they did not take us into the house. The guards led us across the field behind the house towards one of the two huge outbuildings that we had seen from the road. I recognized them as tobacco-curing barns. The roofs and sides were made of timber planks. They were well ventilated for their intended purpose: to dry the large tobacco leaves and store them until they were ready for market.

Once inside, we could see the snowy fields between the gaps in the wall planks, and the winter sky was visible in broad strips where the tops of the walls ended short of the roof. Stacks of metal bed parts and bedding lined one wall. They immediately put us to work assembling the bunk beds that we would sleep in. They gave each of us two blankets and a pillow. About an hour later, an army truck brought food: one bowl of cabbage soup and a single slice of bread. No one complained. We were hungry and grateful for the food.

People continued to arrive, truck loads of them about every half hour. By the time it got dark, I think there must have been 300 of us.

In the next couple of days, both barns filled up, and they started bringing in prefabricated temporary buildings. Our barn had a head count of 752. I remember, because each night at lights-out, we counted off. The guards told us it was for our protection, so that no one got lost. The beds were stacked three high in some places, four high in others. Men, women and children were all together.

Within a few days, a standard menu of food was organized. For breakfast, we had a 20-gram chunk of cheese and a 40-gram slice of bread. At noon we had another slice of bread and a slice of cheap pork sausage, the kind we call polony in Australia, similar to what Americans call baloney. The evening meal was bean soup one day and cabbage soup the next, with a 40-gram slice of bread.

Soon there were somewhere near 3,000 of us. They built a fence around us, three meters high, with 24-hour guards and guard dogs. People who had money were allowed to go out into the town to buy whatever they wanted. They came back with stories of a good-sized Hungarian population in Osijek who were afraid to speak Hungarian. Physical assaults on Hungarians living free in the community were common, and sometimes brutal beatings occurred. Local people were forbidden to talk to people from the camp, but somehow the camp people managed to trade their Hungarian money for food like speck bacon and ham. There was not that much to buy; the local people were very poor, too. Money soon ran out, and within two weeks, I was back to square one. Everybody was the same.

It was the middle of February when representatives from the United Nations made their first visit to our camp. On that day, for the first time, we had meat pieces in our soup. I have never forgotten how nice it was. The entire UN delegation spoke English and had to use interpreters. They interviewed many of us, including me. Some of us complained about being locked up like criminals; everyone complained about the food. We were all sick of cabbage and bean soups. I remember in my interview one of the women from the UN said I was so skinny and asked if I was sick. That was the first time I really took a look at myself since leaving home a month before. My hands were thin and bony, and I could see the outline of my ribs.

The camp's commanding officer was not happy with our complaints. After the UN people left, he called a meeting.

'You have no right to complain,' he shouted in righteous anger. 'You can go to hell or go back to Hungary!'

Few of us would have thought how frustrating it must have been for the Yugoslavs to organize the welfare of so many people on such short notice.

By early March, things started to get better. Every other week we were allowed two hours leave from the camp. For the first time, I left the camp and took the twenty-minute walk to Osijek. I didn't have any money by then or anything to trade, but still it was nice to be free. Unless you are locked up for so long, you don't know how it feels to be free.

About the same time, they started to separate married couples from single men. Maybe there was too much hanky panky going on or maybe this was something the UN people had asked for. I don't remember any physical fighting among us. I think because we were all in the same boat.

The biggest problem in the camp was the toilets. At first, they had three toilets that the women were using all the time, so the men mostly used the field. As the weather warmed up, the smell was so bad that they sprayed the area with lime dust, and we were put to work constructing another toilet area. We dug about fifteen long trenches about one meter deep and put hand rails on both sides. We would hang onto the hand rails and straddle the narrow trench. To keep the smell down, they sprayed it with lime from time to time.

It must be a universal truth that being a prison guard brings out the worst in some people. Nearly every day, we would hear one of them say, 'I hope you all die here.' Some of the guards were brutal, the worst of them always looking for opportunities to deliver a beating. Particularly before the UN came, there were attempts to sneak out to get food or cigarettes. Those who were caught were severely beaten and locked up without food for a day or two.

Another universal truth seems to be that people will find a way to laugh and play in the midst of adversity. We played chess and cards, but the best thing was the music. Our refugee community included one gypsy with a violin and one with a piano accordion. Someone gave me a bucket. I put a towel on the back of it, which muffled the sound of it, and it sounded just like a drum. If I wanted to dance there were always plenty of volunteers to play the drum. We made music every night until the lights switched off.

After lights out, there was one bit of fun left for us young blokes. Our diet of beans and cabbage guaranteed a nightly symphony of farts. Someone came up with the idea that the gas must be flammable. That set off a competition. With a lighted match over our upturned butts, we tried to see who could produce the most spectacular fireworks. Until the novelty wore off, that was always good for a hard laugh that sent us off into a sound sleep.

Too, there were always practical jokes. One time we created an elaborate mock marriage. The bride was a volunteer, but the groom didn't know it was a joke until it was all over. It took all day and I haven't laughed so much since. The man who pretended to conduct the marriage ceremony was very convincing. The poor groom never guessed he was being made the brunt of a joke. He was really upset when he found that, after a whole day's anticipation, he wasn't taking his new bride to bed. We were too starved for mirth to care that we might hurt his feelings.

By the end of May, the weather had warmed enough to create unsafe conditions. Disease breakouts caused the health inspectors from the UN to demand that the Yugoslavs do something about the overcrowding and mounting health problems. Some refugees who had relatives or dual citizenship were released to the countries that had accepted them. It was much later that I learned many of us were being held economic hostage. We had been accepted by one or more of our country choices, but until the UN paid their past-due bills, we weren't allowed to go anywhere.

By this time, some of my friends had returned home, and I had heard stories of how they had been harassed. Then I got a letter from my mother saying it was alright to come back. But I knew I would not be going back to a hero's welcome. Imagine me returning six months later in the same clothes with my ass hanging out. I think I feared the wound to my pride more than I ever feared jail and beatings. So the harder it got, the more I determined to go forward. It wasn't an adventure for me. I simply didn't see any way out, except to just keep going and see what happened.

12

Sheltering in Italy

The UN delegate had promised, 'We will get you out of this hell as soon as possible,' and the next week we were all on trains. Half went to Austria, but I was in the group who boarded the special train that transported us to a camp at Brestanica in the Yugoslavian state of Slovenia. After living in an overcrowded, open-air barn for five months, none of us were prepared for our new surroundings. We stayed in a medieval castle that was once occupied by monks. The castle was on top of a mountain, and the Sava River was a stone's throw away. The castle and the scenery were absolutely beautiful. We still had guards, but we could come and go as we pleased within certain rules. We had to be back at certain times and had set times for eating. If we missed a meal time, too bad. The food was a little bit better, but still mostly cabbage and bean soups.

I slept on the bottom of the double bunk and George, a mate of mine from the first camp, slept above. George wasn't feeling too good when we arrived, and about a week later, he was so sick that I swapped beds with him. He continued to get sicker and sicker and stopped eating.

'Don't worry about me,' he'd say. 'I'll be alright.'

One night he babbled all night, the way someone in a fever does. Nothing he said made sense, and he didn't answer me when I spoke to him. In the morning, I went to the commander's office and spoke with his secretary. Someone from the office came and had a look at him, and not too long after that, a doctor came. They took him away in an ambulance and I never saw him again.

A few days later I was told that he had died with meningitis. I took it hard. I couldn't believe he would just get sick one day and never recover. Everybody in the camp—men, women and children, about 1,500 of us—went to the funeral. I don't know who paid for it, but there were flowers and a beautiful casket. He was buried in the cemetery near the town.

The UN people came to check on us every two or three days. Rumour was that they were going to take us out of the country before it got worse. We were allowed to leave the camp, but nobody had any money or anything to trade with the local people. When we went out to the town, we must have looked really bad, because they didn't want to have anything to do with us. We were all still wearing the same clothes we had been wearing when we left Hungary.

'We must really look like refugees,' we would say to one another, and then laugh. What else could we do? Looking back on it, it's sad to remember that the ones who suffered most were the very young children; some of them looked really bad. When you live in bad conditions, you get used to it until you see others. Only one thing kept me going. I was determined to see the end, to see where it took me. No way I was giving up.

Some people broke down with the waiting and the hunger and the loss of dignity and humanity. Some of them went back to Hungary; others left the camp and stayed on in Yugoslavia. The dream of a better life overseas or in Germany or in Italy was not strong enough to carry them.

We only stayed about three weeks at the castle before we were transported to the railway station on trucks. We got off the train at a place called Sežana, where there was a border station between Yugoslavia and Italy. We were checked by the Yugoslav border guards and then checked by the Italian border guards. The locomotive was changed to an Italian locomotive, and we reboarded and resumed our journey. We arrived early in the morning at Trieste. I think there were about 1,200 of us, and all of us were jumping for joy that we finally had made it.

We were transferred to motor coaches of twelve to fifteen passengers each. It was breakfast time. Priests and nuns came onto the coaches with milk in paper cups and ham rolls, cheese rolls, jam rolls—rolls of every description. My weight had fallen to around 36 kilos, and I ate like a pig. Most of the priests and nuns spoke Hungarian. They were crying when they saw us. I'm not sure if they were crying about the way we looked or that they were happy to see their countrymen.

We were in Trieste for four or five hours. Our train was decorated with flags displaying the old Hungarian emblem with the crown, and then it took off, heading south. At every station, there were people cheering and shouting. We were welcomed as heroes. They must have understood something of what we'd been through; they always offered food.

I was one of four who began to have continuous diarrhea from eating more food than we were accustomed to having. At one station, they picked up medicine for us. It stopped the runs, and we were instructed not to eat anything else. An ambulance met the train in Rome, and the four of us were transported to a nearby hospital. They gave me two injections and some white stuff that tasted like chalk. Apparently there was nothing really seriously wrong, and they got us back to the train just in time. As I began feeling better, I started to enjoy watching the passing countryside outside the train window. News of the special train carrying Hungarian refugees must have reached all the towns up and down the track. In some places, as our train sped by, we would see people standing near the railway line waving to us. I saw lots of vineyards on the way, the grapes already ripening. It was the first time I had ever seen groves of orange trees and lemon trees.

When we got off at Aversa, about forty kilometers south of Naples, we were transported to a huge refugee camp. There must have been thousands of people. We were given bed sheets, a pillow and two blankets and taken to our rooms. There were four beds in the room where I stayed. Not long after we made our beds, we were told it was tea time. We went into a very large room, where we got our plates, cutlery and napkins, and got in line to wait our turn to be served. That was the first time I ever had minced beef and spaghetti. It tasted very good.

The next morning there was coffee, with or without milk, bacon and eggs and one small Vienna loaf. The bread was for all day. If you ate all of it at once, then you went without the rest of the day unless you bought it in the shop. But we had no money.

We were not the only people in the camp. I met people who had been there for months, even years. One man told me he and his wife had been there since 1938. His wife had a history of tuberculosis and no country would take her. 1938! That was the year I was born.

There was a PA system in the camp, and from time to time they called out people's names. On the third day, my name was called to report to the office. They gave me a complete medical check, x-ray, the lot. I was told that I was well underweight for my age and not fit to go on the ship to go to Australia, but if I wanted, I could fly to Canada or the US. I told the doctor that I wanted to go where there was no winter, only sunshine.

That was half the truth. I had been reading the news about race riots in America. I was too young and inexperienced to know that bigotry crosses geographic boundaries as easily as a bird in flight. At the time, I only knew that I had experienced all the racial hatred I thought I could pack into one lifetime, and I didn't want to find myself so soon back into the sadistic melee of cultural intolerance. Because of my insistence that Australia was where I wanted to go, the doctor told me I had to wait at least three months. I said fine. So I had three months to eat hearty and put on weight.

Agents from France and the US were there, trying to recruit young men for military service. The French Foreign Legion was looking for recruits to fight in Morocco. With four years service, a Legionnaire would be granted French citizenship. The US Army offered a very good cash advance, in addition to the promise of US citizenship after four years service in West Germany or in Japan. Another group was recruiting mercenaries to serve in Africa. I did not hesitate to say no to them all. I had had enough of military uniforms, frozen toes, racial curses and hunger. I had already begun to dream of white beaches and endless Australian summers. Two of my friends joined the US Army, one sent to Japan, the other to Germany. We kept in touch for a while, then the letters stopped coming and I stopped writing.

Every morning, my friends and I went into the town to look for odd jobs. We often found work with shop owners in the flea market. We helped to unpack and display the goods, and they paid us very well. We also received pocket money from UN refugee funds, vouchers for free travel on local public transportation and big discounts on train travel. Ticket inspectors never checked for our tickets. They must have taken one look at us and knew we were from the refugee camp.

There was a lot for a tourist to see in Italy, and we had lots of opportunity to travel. We went to Florence, Napoli and Pompeii. We made two or three trips to Rome, where we saw the Vatican and many of the city's famous sights. It was the first time I had seen places where women sold their bodies. It was too great a temptation for a teenage boy from a small Hungarian farm. I tried several times, but they threw me out for being underage.

At the beginning of November, 1957, I was called in for a complete physical examination. I passed! They told me to be ready for departure within two weeks. The excitement was building as I waited until I finally heard my name called again over the big speakers. When I reported to the office, there were officials from Australia and from the UN. They took photographs and had me sign some papers. The next day they gave me a passport issued by the UN Refugee Office, one way only to Australia. I was lucky I had my Hungarian ID. My paperwork was simple, brief and straightforward. Those who had no identification and no travel documents had a mountain of paperwork to overcome.

It was finally happening. I had truly left home.

13

Sailing for Australia

Two days later, two buses picked up those of us who were scheduled for the ocean trip to Australia and dropped us at the railway station. The train left quite late at night, and we arrived very early in the morning at the port of Genoa. Again, they lined us up in a huge shed, checking all our papers. There were thousands of people waiting to board. I received a ticket with all the details, including my room number, then took my place in line, where I waited my turn to board the ship. When I finally walked out of the shed, I stood for a moment, looking for the ship, then realized it was right in front of me. It was two stories high, and I could see its name painted on the hull—*Auralia*. I had never seen a ship so big. I had only seen river boats, and this was an ocean liner.

A steward guided me to my cabin. I had no luggage at all, only the clothes on my back and the papers in my hand. I put all my papers in my pocket and went back up to the deck. There were other, much bigger ships behind us. I saw the *QE2* and the *Oronsay,* which was just as big. The *Auralia* seemed tiny in comparison.

Dinner was served while we were still in dock. I was in heaven. The food was good, served with red and white wine and delivered to our tables. It was quite a change from queuing up for meals in the refugee camp. They treated us like humans. It felt good. The ship left dock close to midnight. It was early December, 1957, and I was only a few short weeks from my first experience on Australian soil.

Some spent the first days hanging over the side, but I was very lucky. I never felt any sign of seasickness. I sold my winter coat to one of the crew members for ten English pounds. We were both happy with the bargain. He had a good winter coat that I never expected I would need in the land of endless summer, and I had some cash.

Our first stop was Malta, where the ship anchored between the two islands. A small boat took us to the main island, where we had seven or eight hours to explore. When we returned to the ship, we found that we had been joined by about a hundred new immigrants bound for Australia.

We arrived at Port Said, at the north entrance of the Suez Canal, on the 19th of December. For over a year, the UK, France and Israel had struggled with Egypt for control of the canal. Egypt had finally won, after threats from the Soviet Union and the United States, who separately but powerfully championed the Egyptian position. The peace had been settled nine months before we arrived, but emotions continued to be raw. As we docked, where we would wait in line until our ship's turn to enter the canal, the captain informed passengers that English, French and the Allies were forbidden to step on shore. The rest of us had four hours to explore the city.

I was shocked to see the way the local people lived, with open sewage on the main street. People would bend down to have a drink from the canal, and the signs of poverty were everywhere. There were beggars on every corner and points in between. They were aggressive in their determination to get something from everyone who passed. I was glad there were four of us so that we could defend ourselves if we needed to.

We came upon a large mosque, by far the nicest building we had seen, and decided to go inside and have a look. As we stepped in, a man quickly came forward and told us that we would have to take off our shoes. We wandered the building, taking our time to admire the intricate designs and patterns that were everywhere. It was very different from anything I had seen before. When we came out, we were again reminded of the awful poverty that was everywhere around us. Our shoes were gone. We walked barefoot the two or three kilometers back to the ship. Most of the ten pounds I received from the sale of my winter jacket went to buy a pair of second-hand shoes from one of the passengers.

The *Auralia* entered the canal as one of a nine-ship convoy. As we made our way through the canal, fighter jets flew overhead. I heard stories on the ship that ours was the first convoy since the end of the Arab-Israeli war. At one point, we anchored in a lake, out of the way of a northbound convoy, then resumed our journey. Sunken ships were visible here and there, a reminder of the recent conflict. There were great crowds of soldiers on the eastern shore of the canal—English, French and, in some places, Israeli. On the west side were the Arabs. The noise from war planes flying in both directions overhead was constant, and from time to time, we were held up by the navies. One time, the captain of the ship warned us that we may have to jump overboard if we were attacked by any of the planes. No one really knew who the enemy was that might attack. And thankfully, we didn't have to find out. We finally emerged from the tunnel of angry faces staring at each other in hatred and the menacing noise of war planes. It had taken all of one day and through the following night.

Once we left Egypt, the sea was very rough for two or three days. We spent most of this time behind closed doors on ship. Nobody went on deck and there were many cases of severe seasickness. When the seas calmed down, one lady, who was quite ill, was taken away by speed boat. I think she may have been sent to Australia later by aeroplane. As we entered the open sea, with the shoreline long out of sight, the ocean became very flat. I often watched the dolphins and the flying fish compete with the ship, racing along beside us. I realized how slowly our ship was moving when other passenger ships that we had left behind in Port Said and Eden began to pass us. The *Auralia* had been a troop carrier for the Italian navy during the war, but it had sunk off the Brazilian coast. After the war, it was refloated and refurbished to carry migrants to Australia. Only a few years later, I heard that it had been sold for scrap.

When we crossed the Equator, the ship slowed down and they told us to look for the red line. Hundreds of us lined the rail and earnestly looked for the red line before we realized it was a joke. The captain ordered the ship to a complete stop and most of us jumped into the ocean to celebrate 'Neptune Day', the crossing of the Equator.

When the fun was over, the ship's engines wouldn't start. It was a beautiful day. I stripped off my shirt, rolled up my pants legs, and stretched out on the top deck. I dozed off in the warm afternoon sun and woke with a jolt to the sound of the engines and the movement of the ship. Five hours had gone by, and I immediately felt the agony of a severe sunburn. A crew member took one look at me and sent me to the ship's hospital. The nurse kept me in for twenty-four hours, putting cream all over my body every couple of hours. When the pain eased, she released me, but for a few more days, I had to report every morning and evening to have more cream applied to my burned skin. After the blisters formed and dissolved, the damaged skin began to come off in big sheets. By the time I landed in Australia, the dead skin had completely peeled off.

14

The Final Refuge

I set foot on Australian soil for the first time in the old port city of Fremantle on the 14th of January, 1958, my twentieth birthday. I had never had a birthday without my family to celebrate with me, but that wasn't the only thing that made this birthday so different. It was the first time in my life I had celebrated a birthday with no snow on the ground. From that day forward, my January birthday would be in the scorching heat of Australian mid-summer.

For hundreds of passengers, this was their destination. The ship remained in port all day, and those of us bound for Melbourne were allowed to get off and look around. Fremantle reminded me of a picturesque Italian village. I got my first taste of Australian weather—and I liked it.

We returned to the ship around six o'clock. At eight o'clock that evening, the ship set out on the final leg of my journey.

The ocean was very rough as we sailed through the Great Australian Bight. For the first time, I joined the line of others hunched over the railing. Once we cleared the Bight, my stomach settled and I began to feel okay.

We arrived at Melbourne midday on the 20th of January. Everybody had to go through customs, then they assembled us into groups. Anyone who had relatives there to meet them were first to disembark, then my group was called. As my group boarded a bus, I had no idea where we were going or what they were going to do with us.

The bus dropped us at a railway station where we boarded a train. Moving from ship to bus to train was no worry at all for me because I had no baggage, just the clothes on my back. Once the train got underway, they handed out sandwiches and a cup of milk. It was a specially scheduled train for the transport of the migrants who had arrived on the *Aurelia*. It stopped once to pick up water for the locomotive and once, in the middle of nowhere, for a red light.

We traveled for hours and hours, and it was very hot. The land looked bare. All I could see were herds of sheep and a few cows. We passed through many small towns, but the train didn't stop. Finally, sometime in the middle of the night, we arrived at our destination. A sign told me I was in Wodonga. Again, we were herded onto buses. There were about ten or twelve of them lined up, and as each bus filled, it took off into the darkness.

This time the journey wasn't so long. The bus turned off the bitumen road and drove into what looked like an army camp, stopping outside a huge reception building.

There were electric lights everywhere; it was like daylight. We walked into a big hall where I had to wait with the rest until my name was called. We were processed alphabetically. So because there were so many, and my name started with 'V', I had to wait well over an hour. When my name was finally called, I was paired with one of my countrymen, a bloke named Sandor. We were taken to a building and shown to a room with two single beds. This time, we did not have to assemble beds or even dress them. They were already comfortably made up with clean sheets, blankets and pillows. After all the activity, we were too wide awake to go right to bed; we decided to walk around and see the camp.

The sun was just coming up. A sign told us we were in Camp Bonegilla, a cluster of barracks-style buildings built during World War II to house Italian prisoners of war. It was odd to think that the Italians who had been so kind to us had once been housed here as prisoners.

As it became full daylight, we noticed people all walking in the same direction towards a big building. I stopped someone to ask where everyone was going. The big building, as it turned out, was the dining hall. Breakfast was being served.

As we entered, the odor of sheep was so strong that it was almost sickening. We were served lamb chops, sausages and fried eggs. It tasted very good to me, and as time went on, I grew accustomed to the smell. That was a good thing because we had a tasty mutton stew almost every day and sometimes lamb or mutton at the other two meals as well.

Similar to the camp in Italy, Bonegilla had a PA system that shouted out the names of people in the camp who needed to report for their next level of processing. My name had been called out, and with some of the people I had met on the ship, I made my way to the sport hall next to the building where we had eaten our breakfast. There were six or seven tables and an officer guided me to one of them, where a woman was seated with a big book before her. Speaking in Hungarian, she asked for my name. She studied the book, found my name, ticked it off with her pencil, and handed me 5 pounds 7 shillings. She explained that once the ship reached Australian waters, I had become entitled to unemployment benefits. She wrote down the amount and showed how she had deducted the cost of accommodation in the camp.

After giving me this accounting, she fell silent for a moment and then politely asked, 'Do you have a change of clothes?'

'No,' I explained, 'I wash my shirt and trousers every other night and my underpants during the day.'

She started laughing and just couldn't seem to stop. When she could finally talk, she gave me the name of someone I should go and see at the camp store. He gave me one shirt, two pairs of socks and a pair of trousers. The only trousers that fit me were ladies' trousers that had zips on both sides. I settled for what I could get. The clothes I had been wearing were falling apart.

So that's how I started in Australia, with a five-pound note plus change and a pair of ladies' trousers. I stayed in the camp for about two weeks, hitchhiking into Wodonga or Albury to have a look around. I did find it very strange that the pubs in Albury stayed open until ten o'clock at night, but Wodonga pubs closed at six o'clock, when it was still daylight. Of course, that affected everything else—delis, shops, everything. That's when I learned that Albury was located in New South Wales and Wodonga was in Victoria, and that different states could have different rules.

During those two weeks, I had job interviews with some of the companies who came to the camp to recruit workers. I wasn't interested in farm work, but I was very interested in a job offer from Australian Iron and Steel. I was in for a long wait, though. They could not take me until they could find accommodation for me, and at the time, all the workers' hostels were full. Some of the local farmers were desperate for fruit pickers, and those of us who had to wait for our permanent jobs were asked if we wanted to help out the farmers for about three months.

The farmers knew about our situation, and the money was good for anyone willing to work. It was piece work: the more you picked, the more you earned. I jumped at the chance to earn some money and to have something to do. I was one of about two hundred who boarded a special train to Robinvale in the early morning dark. We arrived to the sight of rows and rows of cars and a crowd of farmers. They moved through the crowd of us and began choosing. It looked like market day when farmers choose sheep for their flocks.

I was in a group of five chosen by a farmer who herded us into his new yellow FE Holden. That was the first time in my short life that I had been inside a new car. The odor of newness was completely foreign to me.

It was daylight by now, and we were speeding along a dirt road, leaving a huge red cloud behind us. There was nothing but vineyards on both sides of the road.

We introduced ourselves and I attempted to make conversation. I would speak a few words of English and the farmer would respond. I don't remember the farmer's name; I'll just call him Jones. The funny thing is that he understood me, but I and my friends didn't understand him. I realized later that we did not understand the simplest English slang. I would say 'do not' and Jones would say 'don't'. We didn't know they meant the same thing.

After about an hour's drive, we drove into his farm on a long dirt driveway. By this time, the sun was well up and it was hot. I thought I would pass out from the heat. Jones showed us to our sleeping quarters, using a combination of English words and gestures that we had worked out to communicate. It was a shed with five beds, a shower and an electric jug to make tea or coffee. We dropped our bags by our beds, and he took us to the house and introduced us to his wife and children—a little girl about four years old and a little boy about seven or eight. He motioned for us to take seats at the kitchen table, and his wife served our breakfast. For the first time, I tasted tea with milk. It tasted really bad that first time, but after a few days I got used to it. My life had become a parade of unfamiliar details that I had to get used to. But the months of bad food, and too little of it, had prepared me well for appreciating the foreign food that I was now offered.

While we were eating, we tried very hard to speak to each other. Jones wanted to know our nationality and everything about us. He told us that he had two more kids, a boy and a girl, the boy at uni and the girl at a boarding school in Melbourne. We learned we would have the day off to settle in and recover from our trip. Work would commence the next day at daylight. If we slept in, Jones explained, he would wake us. It wasn't a warning, but an assurance. He was a good bloke.

By lunch time of our day of arrival, it was so hot that I felt dizzy. After lunch Jones took us to the vineyard to see what we would be doing. We had to pick the grapes—not just the big bunches but all bunches—and put them in boxes about the size of milk crates. I think we were paid 2 shillings, 6 pence per box. After the first week, we had every Sunday off. On Sunday, we washed our work clothes. We worked sun up to sundown, six days a week. The job was easy, but it was hot between the rows of grape vines.

We had been at our job as grape pickers for about four weeks when we woke up on a Saturday morning and it was pouring rain. Jones told us that we didn't have to work. It was good to have a break. Late in the morning, he stepped into our shed. There was nothing to do, and we were sitting on our beds making idle conversation.

'You blokes want to come into town with me?' he asked.

We understood that!

Our first stop was the pub, and Jones bought each of us a large glass of beer. I wasn't a beer drinker, but it was so cold I really enjoyed it. He bought us hot dogs, the first time I'd ever tasted one. Actually, it was the first time I had ever heard about one. I wondered why they called it 'hot dog'. We walked around a bit, and Jones pointed out various buildings.

I'm guessing that he was telling us what they were. We nodded and said yes to everything. We didn't understand anything he was saying. I think he suspected, but just kept on talking and pointing.

The first thing we really understood was when he asked if we would like to see a football match. Of course we said yes. We walked a few hundred meters until we reached a park. It didn't look like a football ground, but there were timbers set up as bench seats, so we sat down. Some people just sat on the ground, some sat on cars and others were standing. A few minutes later, about fifty players ran onto the middle of the oval-shaped field. It started to rain again but they continued to play. One of them carried an egg-shaped ball.

My mate poked me in the ribs with his elbow. 'Look,' he said, 'the poor players can't afford to buy a proper ball!'

Suddenly all of them started punching each other, and some other men ran onto the grounds and tried to stop the fight. The rain was pouring and they were totally covered with mud and blood. A few more plays and we realized this wasn't proper football. It was some other game altogether.

'This country is full of surprises,' I said to my mate at the end of the game.

We laughed and shook hands and hugged each other. What would be next in this land where football was a free-for-all fight, played with an odd-shaped ball by gangs of young ruffians?

After we finished our grape picking for Jones, I took on a few other small jobs, then went back to Bonegilla in Victoria. It was three weeks later, in early June, when about twenty of us were put on the train to Wollongong. We were again met by a bus that was intended only for our transport. It was about a half hour's drive to the Unanderro Hostel in New South Wales. We were directed to a huge hall and waited there until our names were called. Again, because my name started with 'V', I was almost the last person to be called. The last four of us were taken up the hill to buildings that looked like a huge 200-liter drum sawed in half the long way, and each half turned upside down. Each building had four rooms, two rooms at each end. They were really nice rooms, each with two simple beds, neatly made up, ready for sleeping. It was the 10th of June, 1958.

The next morning, a man came to my room and guided me to a small bus. Some of my mates were already on board. There were no farms in view as we traveled, just one factory after another popping up on both sides of the road. We finally arrived at a gate where a big sign announced that we were at 'Australian Iron and Steel'. Below, a smaller sign said 'Hoskins Kembla Works'. There was a lot of activity and it was very noisy. After checking our names against a list, we were sent to have medical checks. They checked everything—x-rays, the works. Afterwards, we lined up outside the medical centre. There were about twenty in the queue, all Hungarians. We sat in the back of a small truck, which transported us to a big storeroom. In turn, I was fitted with safety boots, a safety helmet, a pair of gloves, safety glasses, a wet-weather coat and leggings. We each signed a receipt for our work gear. That was when we learned that we would be paid double time because it was the Queen's Birthday, a public holiday in New South Wales.

Again, we had to line up and we were asked if any of us spoke English. The man didn't say how much English, so I put up my hand. I don't know about the other bloke who put up his hand, but I only knew maybe a dozen words. The rest of them had to climb up on the truck and were taken away. The two of us stood there, waiting, about five minutes, then an old ex-army Land Rover pulled up. The driver told us to get in. It was lunch time, and he drove us to a small criproom, where we ate our sandwiches supplied by the hostel. We got back into the Land Rover and were taken from one side of the steel works to the other side of the main road. After a short time, I could see the ocean. I kept thinking to myself, 'Where are we going?' Then suddenly he stopped at a small shed between the railway lines on the jetty and motioned for me to get out. He stepped out of the Land Rover, handed me a pencil and a small writing pad, and began talking to me, occasionally waving his hands towards the passing trucks. I was certain he was explaining what I was to do, but I didn't understand a bloody word. Every time he looked at me, I would say, 'Yes, yes,' but I had no idea what he was talking about. I stood in front of the little shed for about an hour. There were trucks running back and forth. Every time one passed they waved at me with a big smile, so I waved back.

Before too long, the Land Rover showed up again, but with a different driver. He got out and approached me, asking me something in English. I just stood there and he must have seen that I didn't understand any of it, so he asked me what nationality I was. I told him that I was Hungarian. Lucky for me, he was too, and he explained to me in Hungarian what it was I was supposed to be doing. The trucks were carrying iron ore from the ship, and he showed me to draw a vertical line each time a truck went by. After four trucks went by, I was to draw a horizontal line through the four vertical lines when the fifth truck came by. Every now and then I was supposed to send a truck to the weight bridge, because they were contractors being paid on average weight.

So that was my very first job at the steel works—twelve hours in every shift and double pay on public holidays. I did that for six weeks, six days a week. I liked the job, but I didn't like the hours, so I wanted out of it; I wanted more time to get out and do things besides work. They put me in the so-called main yard department, and I worked most days in different areas of the steel works. For a twenty year old, eight hours a day was perfect.

15

Strangers in a Strange Land

The Uanderra Hostel was in Woolongong, an eastern suburb of Sydney. Cringalla, Port Kambla and Woolongong were full of coffee lounges where migrants of different nationalities got together because most of us spoke very little English. Every evening you got rid of your frustration of not speaking all day at work. Human beings are very keen to communicate and get rid of the loneliness. Rooms for single people at the hostel were tiny—two by three meters with two people in the room. Uanderra Hostel had both single quarters and family quarters, separated by about 500 meters. There was a common dining room. You were allowed to stay in the hostel for two years. From then on, you had to find your own way.

Financially, we all bettered ourselves, but emotionally a lot of people went through hell. There were people who just broke down. Single men often turned to heavy drinking or heavy gambling. I think they must have looked at themselves and saw it was too late to go back where they came from, and the misery of it drug them down. They finished up in debt, and some of them took the easy way out with suicide.

I knew one bloke whose wife went off with a younger man and left him with four children. He shot himself. I never found out what happened to the kids.

One day I was at the SP betting with a very close friend of mine. He put 80 pounds on one of the horses and told us if he lost he was going to hang himself. We all laughed. No one saw him for about a week after that. Then the news came that a bloke from the railway had got caught in the rain and ducked into a shed on the side of the hill, and there he found the body of my friend. It had hung so long that the head had separated from the body. He and I had travelled together to Sydney a lot. He had a permanent job in the steel works, he was well liked, always joking, no sign of mental depression that I could see. We became good friends because neither of us were drinkers. I had no idea.

Another friend just went to sleep one night and didn't wake up. They said it was some sort of overdose. He had a new car, no sign of depression. We never got the whole story because we were not relatives. We just grieved because he died and didn't think about how or why he died.

I always missed my family, and when I had to eat in cafés and restaurants, I especially longed for my mother's cooking.

I think immigration is hardest on married couples and families. There were so many single men who wanted to get laid. It was very attractive to a woman who had kids. Her husband worked. A single man had the same pay and could buy a new car and tempt her with luxuries. I, myself, just took them out with nice music, nightclub, whatever, while the poor bloke was working his bloody arse off. For a woman, it was just to get out of the damned place. They had no English, and all they could do was just window shop. The men learned English a lot quicker because of the work situation. You just had to learn the basic words to work.

My best friend took on a woman who was about eight years older than him and had six kids. Her husband worked shift work. Over time, they became friends and then grew very close. Eventually they kicked the husband out and still happily live together to this day.

I was living the happy life of a single man. By day I worked in the steel works, and by night I played in a band. My English finally became good enough that I could understand anyone and they could mostly understand me. As a band musician and with my heavy Hungarian accent, young girls seemed to find me a romantic figure, and I did not mind taking advantage of it. But one night in the club where I was playing, I met a Polish beauty with long legs and large, blue eyes. She, too, has a story to tell. Her parents met in a Polish displaced persons camp midst the European rubble of World War II.

But that is all history. Today we have a daughter and a son, grandchildren, and even great grandchildren.

Now we are Australian, and as so many other Australians, no longer refugees. Even my family in Hungary have stopped running to seek refuge. Their lands have been restored, and they live ordinary lives in warm, comfortable homes with plenty to eat. We all believe that we are home safe. But then so did those German families who lived in Hungary for two hundred years until a shift in political power redefined their boundaries of safety. Perhaps we human beings are a race of refugees, most of us running from one place to the next, seeking to escape the ambitions of those whose lives are devoted to the manufacture, maintenance and transfer of power.